Early Settlement and Subsistence in the Casma Valley, Peru

EARLY SETTLEMENT AND SUBSISTENCE IN THE CASMA VALLEY, PERU

By Shelia Pozorski and Thomas Pozorski

UNIVERSITY OF IOWA PRESS Ψ IOWA CITY

University of Iowa Press, Iowa City 52242
Copyright © 1987 by the University of Iowa
All rights reserved
Printed in the United States of America
First edition, 1987

Typesetting by G&S Typesetters, Austin, Texas
Printing and binding by Braun-Brumfield,
Ann Arbor, Michigan

Library of Congress Cataloging-in-Publication
Data

Pozorski, Shelia Griffis.
 Early settlement and subsistence in the
Casma Valley, Peru.

  Bibliography: p.
  Includes index.
  1. Indians of South America—Peru—
Casma River Valley—Antiquities. 2. Casma
River Valley (Peru)—Antiquities. 3. In-
dians of South America—Peru—Casma River
Valley—Economic conditions. 4. Peru—
Antiquities. I. Pozorski, Thomas George.
II. Title.
F3429.1.C37P69 1988   985'.21   87-25517
 ISBN 0-87745-183-4

Contents

Acknowledgments

Permission to excavate in the Casma Valley was granted by the Peruvian Instituto Nacional de Cultura, and funding for survey and excavation was provided by grants from the O'Neil and Netting Funds of Carnegie Museum of Natural History. Funds for the radiocarbon assays were provided by grant BNS-8203452 from the National Science Foundation. Special thanks go to Stanley Lantz and Edmund Dlutowski, who helped with excavations at the sites of Pampa de las Llamas-Moxeke and San Diego and also participated in the laboratory analysis. We also extend our appreciation to George Harlow and Edmund Dlutowski, who performed analyses on the mortar at Las Haldas. Figure 6 is based on a map of Las Haldas published by Terence Grieder (1975), which we subsequently modified on the basis of our observations and excavations. The field drawing of figure 32 was made by Edmund Dlutowski, and figures 10, 11, 36, 37, 55, and 63 were drawn by Felix Farro. Margaret Adams printed many of the photographs. We would also like to thank our reviewers for their many suggestions for improving the manuscript.

Early Settlement and Subsistence in the Casma Valley, Peru

Introduction

Our interest in the Casma Valley dates from 1974 when, inspired by the descriptions of Tello (1956) and Kosok (1965), we first visited the valley. Until 1979, our visits were sporadic—accomplished at free moments during our investigations of the Moche Valley to the north. In 1979 and 1980, funding provided by the O'Neil and Netting Funds of Carnegie Museum of Natural History made it possible for us to carry out surveys and test excavations at selected sites within and near the Casma Valley. This publication presents the preliminary results of those 1979 and 1980 investigations. Once all data have been more thoroughly analyzed and evaluated, a final report will be prepared.

ENVIRONMENTAL SETTING

The Peruvian coast is one of the driest deserts in the world. Rain is scarce because of the cold Peruvian or Humboldt Current that flows south to north from northern Chile to northern Peru. The cold waters of this current keep the air over the ocean cold and hold evaporation to a minimum. As the air moves inland, it is warmed and its capacity to hold water is increased, but rain does not fall until the air reaches the cooler elevations of the Andes at altitudes above 2,500 meters.

Although the coast is kept arid by the Peruvian Current, it is also blessed with the richest oceanic biomass in the world. The continuous upwelling of nutrient-rich cold waters from depths below supports a tremendous food chain of plankton, shellfish, fish, seabirds, and sea mammals. These marine resources played a vital part in the development of coastal Andean civilization and are still important today.

A few times every century, a large portion of the cold Peruvian Current is temporarily displaced by the warm Ecuadorian Countercurrent, resulting in a phenomenon called El Niño. When a severe El Niño occurs, as it did in 1925 and 1983, the marine food chain is affected, and torrential rains drench the coastal desert. These effects occur in decreasing intensity toward the south, depending on the magnitude of the El Niño phenomenon.

By the time of the earliest occupation of the sites dealt with in this study (after 3000 B.C.), both climate and sea level had stabilized and were close to modern conditions (Craig and Psuty 1968; Osborn 1977; Parsons 1970). Therefore, the general conditions described above for contemporary Peru are applicable to the periods of cultural development we have chosen to investigate.

The Casma Valley, one of fifty-seven river valleys that cross the Peruvian desert coast, is located on the north-central coast some 350 kilometers north of Lima (fig. 1). The valley (fig. 2) actually consists of two rivers, the Sechin branch on the north and the Casma branch on the south, which meet to form the Casma River some 10 kilometers from the Pacific Ocean. The total drainage basin is 2,775 square kilometers, but like most Peruvian coastal rivers, the Casma River is characterized by marked seasonal variation in river flow. The peak flow period, December to April, has monthly runoff rates up to 89 cubic meters per second (ONERN 1972: 31, 290). Since rain almost never falls on the Peruvian coast, all agriculture is dependent on canal irrigation, making river flow extremely important.

Both branches of the Casma Valley are bordered by steep mountains and are rather narrow, varying from 1.5 to 2 kilometers wide, until they join to form the Casma Valley proper. Near this junction, the surrounding mountains become smaller foothills, often interspersed with stretches of desert sands, and the Casma Valley widens to 7 kilometers near its mouth. Within a few kilometers of the area of the mouth, land is only a few meters above sea level and is often too salty for agricultural purposes.

PROJECT OBJECTIVES

General surveys had already been done in the lower Casma Valley by Collier (1962) and Thompson (1961, 1962a, 1964a, 1974), and well up-valley within the Sechin branch of the Casma Valley by Fung and Williams (1977). Since our previous investigations in the Moche Valley at early sites had yielded important new findings (S. Pozorski 1976, 1979; S. Pozorski and T. Pozorski 1979a, 1979b; T. Pozorski 1975, 1976), and since the Casma Valley contains the largest concentration of Cotton Preceramic, Initial Period, and Early Horizon sites along the north and central Peruvian coast, we felt our best potential for contribution would

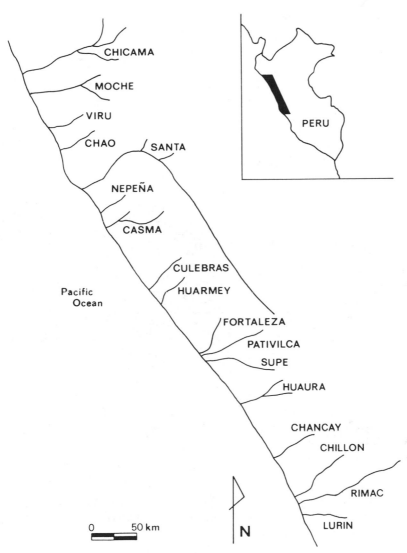

Fig. 1. River valleys along the north and central coast of Peru.

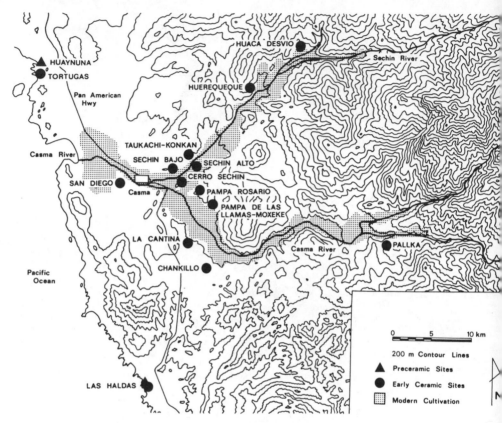

Fig. 2. Locations of Cotton Preceramic, Initial Period, and Early Horizon sites in the Casma Valley.

lie in the intensive investigation of major early Casma Valley sites.

Our study had three main objectives. Our first goal was the chronological placement of each of the major early sites based on recovered artifacts, architectural data, and available absolute dates. Second, we planned to study subsistence changes through time. Our third objective was dependent on the first two: we hoped to understand the processual development of early Casma Valley society.

To accomplish these objectives, we excavated at six sites in the Casma Valley area: Huaynuná, Las Haldas, Pampa de las Llamas-Moxeke, Tortugas, San Diego, and Pampa Rosario. We also intensively surveyed additional early sites. In selecting sites for excavation, we attempted to sample sites dating to all three major early time periods: Cotton Preceramic (2500–1800 B.C.), Initial Period (1800–900 B.C.), and Early Horizon (900–200 B.C.). Local preservation was also a factor, since this investigation had a subsistence focus. We gave high priority to sites in immediate danger of destruction, such as Tortugas, which is already badly damaged by a resort development, and Pampa Rosario, which has lost several major structures to modern canal and road construction. Finally, accessibility was a factor. Since time and money were limited, we tested none of the very remote upvalley sites. The excavated sites include two with Cotton Preceramic components: Huaynuná and preceramic Las Haldas; two sites which we believed to be Initial Period: Pampa de las Llamas-Moxeke and Tortugas, as well as the ceramic component of Las Haldas; and two which appeared to date to the Early Horizon: San Diego and Pampa Rosario. Las Haldas is a key site in this study because it represents a lengthy occupation which spanned all of these time periods.

We have partially realized all three objectives. Ceramics, artifactual data, and radiocarbon dates from excavations have been correlated with architectural evidence from both survey and excavation to create a tentative chronology for the early periods of Casma Valley prehistory (table 1). Although we tested some sites more extensively than others, we made at least one controlled stratigraphic excavation to collect subsistence remains at each site. Every site yielded floral and faunal material, and the analysis of the domesticated plant species by specialists is well underway.

Drawing on all these sources—excavations in architecture, recovered artifacts, radiocarbon dates, survey data, and specialized subsistence studies—we have begun to reconstruct Casma Valley development. The period between 2500 and 200 B.C. was characterized by three especially significant events. First, there is evidence that the most spectacular developments during all of Casma Valley prehistory occurred during the Initial Period. Initial Period sites contrast markedly with their Cotton Preceramic antecedents, but there are clear continuities between the two periods as well. Second, there is almost no continuity between the Initial Period polity centers and subsequent Casma Valley settlements because the Initial Period florescence was abruptly truncated by an invasion from the highlands. The third major event involved the settlement of the lower Casma Valley by the conquerors during the Early Horizon. These new people brought about a drastic change in the local life-style.

The following report describes the major results of our investigations

TABLE 1. Chronological Placement of Early Sites of the Casma Valley, Peru

Cotton Preceramic	Initial Period
2500 B.C. 1800 B.C.	
HUAYNUNÁ—————	
LAS HALDAS—————	
	PAMPA DE LAS—————————————
	LLAMAS-MOXEKE
	TORTUGAS—————————————————
	SECHIN ALTO————————————————
	CERRO SECHIN—————————————————
	HUEREQUEQUE—————————————
	PALLKA—————————
	SECHIN BAJO—————
	TAUKACHI-
	KONKAN—————————

and consists of four chapters. Following the introduction, which provides background material, the second chapter presents the results of fieldwork at the six sites where excavations were realized: Huaynuná, Las Haldas, Pampa de las Llamas-Moxeke, Tortugas, San Diego, and Pampa Rosario. The third chapter consists of our observations based on survey at the sites of Huerequeque, Sechin Alto, Taukachi-Konkan, Sechin Bajo, Cerro Sechin, Pallka, Huaca Desvio, Chankillo, and La Cantina. The fourth chapter reviews sequences proposed by earlier investigators for early Casma Valley sites and outlines our detailed new sequence for Casma Valley prehistory. It concludes with a summary of the data and conclusions pertinent to this new interpretation of Casma Valley prehistory and attempts to relate them to other developments in the Andean area.

Early Horizon

900 B.C.   200 B.C.

PAMPA ROSARIO————————————

HUACA DESVIO————————————

SAN DIEGO————————————

LA CANTINA————————————

CHANKILLO————————————

2

Casma Valley Sites Excavated in 1980

From July through October of 1980, we were able to conduct a series of test pits, stratigraphic excavations, and limited architectural clearings at six early sites in the Casma Valley area. This chapter presents the results of these investigations. Since we followed the same excavation procedures at all of the sites, the methodology we used is described once, before the discussions of discoveries made at each site.

The sections on the results of our investigations are generally arranged chronologically by site. First we discuss the Cotton Preceramic Period site of Huaynuná. This is followed by a section on Las Haldas, which has a Cotton Preceramic component. For the sake of clarity, however, we also describe the Initial Period and Early Horizon occupations of Las Haldas in this same section. The remaining sites are essentially single-component sites and are presented in a straightforward chronological manner. The Initial Period sites of Pampa de las Llamas-Moxeke and Tortugas are discussed after Las Haldas, followed by the Early Horizon sites of San Diego and Pampa Rosario.

METHODOLOGY

The primary objectives of our 1980 field season were to obtain information on chronology and subsistence. A secondary objective was to explore briefly architectural features at each site containing evidence of structures. To accomplish our primary goals, we concentrated our efforts in midden areas of each site where we expected to find the best stratigraphic deposition available for chronological and subsistence studies. Since time and money were limited, the most efficient manner of locating the deepest and richest refuse deposits was to place a series of small 1-by-1-meter test pits in areas that looked most promising on the basis of surface evidence. Each test pit was dug rapidly, and the excavator saved artifacts and subsistence items as he excavated the pit.

Once each pit was completed, the variety and quantity of artifacts and subsistence items were noted, as was the general nature and condition of the stratigraphy in the side walls of the test pit. Once all test pits at a site were completed, the results were compared and certain pits selected for expansion into controlled stratigraphic excavations.

With few exceptions, each controlled stratigraphic excavation had areal dimensions of 1 meter by 1 meter. Since each one was extended off a previous test pit, the stratigraphy of one side of the cut was clearly visible prior to excavation. This enabled excavation to proceed by natural levels, with each level being carefully followed from the front of the cut toward the back. In the cases where natural levels were unusually thick, these were subdivided into smaller arbitrary levels, usually 10 centimeters thick or less. All excavated soil was passed through a 1/4-inch screen, which was lightly tapped instead of scraped so that delicate plant remains would not be crushed as soil was moved over the screen surface. In addition to being passed through the 1/4-inch screen, a 25-centimeter square column from each cut was passed through two sizes of successively finer mesh screen (2-millimeter and 710-micrometer openings respectively) in order to obtain samples of small seeds and bones that ordinarily pass through the 1/4-inch screen.

Charcoal for radiocarbon dating was collected from natural levels or parts of natural levels as controlled stratigraphic excavations progressed. Table 2 lists the dates that we obtained from the six Casma Valley sites excavated, and also provides contextual data for each sample. Column 6, Stratigraphic Excavation Unit, refers to the numbered cuts represented by square symbols on the plans of each excavated site. Column 7 lists the natural level below the ground surface. For example, 6a refers to approximately the upper 10 centimeters of deposit within the sixth natural level below the surface. Column 8 indicates the minimum and maximum depths below the surface at which the natural level occurs. Wide ranges are indicative of the uneven, often sharply sloping nature of natural strata and *do not* signify that any level is well over 10 centimeters thick. Finally, the numbers in Column 9 give the depth to which the cut was excavated. In most cases this is the depth of the boundary between artifact-bearing strata and sterile substrate, but some samples from Tortugas and Las Haldas ended at such cultural boundaries as floors or platform surfaces.

We made a preliminary analysis of the subsistence remains in Peru, and we brought samples of many of the important plant food species to the United States for analysis by specialists. Most have been identified,

TABLE 2. Casma Valley Radiocarbon Dates

Site	Sample Number	Material	Radiocarbon Years
Huaynuná	UGA-4522	charcoal	4200 ± 80[1]
Huaynuná	UGA-4520	charcoal	4040 ± 65
Huaynuná	UGA-4521	charcoal	3725 ± 75
Precer. Las Haldas	UGA-4531	charcoal	3960 ± 80
Precer. Las Haldas	UGA-4529	charcoal	3785 ± 60
Precer. Las Haldas	UGA-4530	charcoal	3745 ± 60
I. Per. Las Haldas	UGA-4534	charcoal	3595 ± 75
I. Per. Las Haldas	UGA-4532	charcoal	3460 ± 75
I. Per. Las Haldas	UGA-4533	charcoal	3140 ± 75
E. Hor. Las Haldas	UGA-4526	charcoal	2990 ± 75
E. Hor. Las Haldas	UGA-4527	charcoal	2915 ± 60
E. Hor. Las Haldas	UGA-4528	charcoal	2845 ± 80
P. Llamas-Moxeke	UGA-4510	charcoal	4655 ± 95
P. Llamas-Moxeke	UGA-4505	charcoal	3735 ± 75
P. Llamas-Moxeke	UGA-4506	charcoal	3490 ± 75
P. Llamas-Moxeke	UGA-4508	charcoal	3425 ± 75
P. Llamas-Moxeke	UGA-4507	charcoal	3390 ± 150
P. Llamas-Moxeke	UGA-4509	charcoal	3220 ± 85
P. Llamas-Moxeke	UGA-4511	charcoal	3175 ± 90
P. Llamas-Moxeke	UGA-4503	charcoal	3165 ± 75
P. Llamas-Moxeke	UGA-4504	charcoal	3070 ± 85
Tortugas	UGA-4524	charcoal	4540 ± 200
Tortugas	UGA-4523	charcoal	4065 ± 65
Tortugas	UGA-4525	charcoal	3750 ± 65
San Diego	UGA-4514	charcoal	2510 ± 115
San Diego	UGA-4512	charcoal	2490 ± 60
San Diego	UGA-4517	charcoal	2455 ± 70
San Diego	UGA-4513	charcoal	2305 ± 55
San Diego	UGA-4516	charcoal	2245 ± 60
Pampa Rosario	UGA-4535	charcoal	2760 ± 75
Pampa Rosario	UGA-4537	charcoal	2535 ± 75
Pampa Rosario	UGA-4536	charcoal	2400 ± 70

[1] All dates are uncorrected based on the Libby Half-life of 5570 ± 30 years.
[2] Depth measured below the compact surface which separates the Initial Period and Cotton Preceramic components.
[3] Depth of Cotton Preceramic component only.

Calendar Years	Stratigraphic Excavation Unit	Natural Level below Surface	Approx. Depth below Surface	Total Depth of Excav. Unit
2250 ± 80 B.C.	1	6a	95–127 cm	164 cm
2090 ± 65 B.C.	1	2b	17–34 cm	164 cm
1775 ± 75 B.C.	1	3c	43–62 cm	164 cm
2010 ± 80 B.C.	1	4d	107–129 cm[2]	169 cm[3]
1835 ± 60 B.C.	1	2b	19–29 cm[2]	169 cm[3]
1795 ± 60 B.C.	1	3c	79–91 cm[2]	169 cm[3]
1645 ± 75 B.C.	2	13	113–149 cm	149 cm
1510 ± 75 B.C.	2	5b	13–39 cm	149 cm
1190 ± 75 B.C.	2	12	103–133 cm	149 cm
1040 ± 75 B.C.	3	2	0–27 cm	170 cm
965 ± 60 B.C.	3	11	74–92 cm	170 cm
895 ± 80 B.C.	3	19	119–144 cm	170 cm
2705 ± 95 B.C.	6	2(Sq. 2)	4–23 cm	71 cm
1785 ± 75 B.C.	3	1a	0–12 cm	49 cm
1540 ± 75 B.C.	3	3	18–32 cm	49 cm
1475 ± 75 B.C.	4	5	18–40 cm	40 cm
1440 ± 150 B.C.	4	2	4–20 cm	40 cm
1370 ± 85 B.C.	6	8(Sq. 1)	34–60 cm	66 cm
1225 ± 90 B.C.	6	10(Sq. 2)	59–67 cm	71 cm
1215 ± 75 B.C.	2	2b	24–59 cm	115 cm
1120 ± 85 B.C.	2	4a	77–100 cm	115 cm
2590 ± 200 B.C.	1	8	65–93 cm	117 cm
2115 ± 65 B.C.	1	4b	36–61 cm	117 cm
1800 ± 65 B.C.	2	6	24–65 cm	102 cm
560 ± 115 B.C.	1	12b	82–98 cm	99 cm
540 ± 60 B.C.	1	4	30–54 cm	99 cm
505 ± 70 B.C.	4	8c	91–130 cm	130 cm
355 ± 55 B.C.	1	11	58–76 cm	99 cm
295 ± 60 B.C.	4	3b	26–47 cm	130 cm
810 ± 75 B.C.	1	7	6–58 cm	150 cm
585 ± 75 B.C.	1	9d	88–109 cm	150 cm
450 ± 70 B.C.	1	8a	22–69 cm	150 cm

but determination of the species represented by fragmentary remains, especially in the case of tubers, has required special study (see Ugent et al. 1981, 1982, 1983, 1984, 1986). Of the faunal remains, shellfish were identified in Peru, whereas samples of fish and mammals were brought to the United States for study. Because analyses of some plant samples as well as the fish bones are not complete, our discussions of subsistence for each site are necessarily preliminary, since precise quantifications cannot be made.

These preliminary discussions focus on what we consider significant species—species which occur consistently within most natural levels of each stratigraphic excavation. We go a step further and rate the relative abundance of these significant species within each cut by using such terms as *abundant, moderately abundant,* and *relatively rare.* Since all the data are not yet available, we are not prepared to discuss changes in species frequencies within each site. However, we can say that there is no evidence for significant intrasite changes in the *inventory* of plant and animal species utilized, except among the three components at Las Haldas, which are clearly distinguishable as separate occupations at a single locus. The few exceptions which are not attributable to rarity are discussed on an individual basis within the text.

To accomplish our secondary objective of sampling architecture, we partially delineated architectural configurations by trenching along wall faces visible on the surface. At Pampa de las Llamas-Moxeke, we were also able to clear entirely a few small rooms within the domestic structures. We also occasionally encountered buried architecture in the midden areas that we excavated.

HUAYNUNÁ

The Cotton Preceramic site of Huaynuná (or Huaynuma) was discovered by Collier (1962: 411) and subsequently tested by Engel (1957a: 56, 1957b: 74–75), who felt it was a seasonal fishing station. It lies some 13 kilometers north of the Casma Valley (fig. 2), in a protected area near the south end of Huaynuná Bay, a sandy arc of beach which is bordered on both the north and south by rocky arms of Andean foothills. Thus both sandy and rocky littoral habitats are easily accessible from the site. Huaynuná covers an area of about 8.5 hectares and extends from near the modern shoreline to about 20 meters above sea level.

We excavated a total of sixteen test pits at Huaynuná to expose both suspected architecture and subsistence remains. We enlarged one test pit, and it formed the base for a 1-square-meter excavation by natural levels that allowed us to examine plant and animal remains in detail. Three radiocarbon dates from charcoal recovered from this stratigraphic excavation, 2250 ± 80 B.C. (UGA-4522), 2090 ± 65 B.C. (UGA-4520), and 1775 ± 75 B.C. (UGA-4521), confirm the site's placement in the late Cotton Preceramic Period (table 2).

Architecture

Huaynuná is distinguishable on the surface as a concentration of very dark ash scattered with marine shell (fig. 3). Few architectural remains are visible, the most notable being traces of walls in the far southwest portion of the site. Testing showed that this architecture dates to early ceramic times. Engel may have noticed this when he compared the architecture of Huaynuná to the small, low-walled domestic structures of Los Chinos at the mouth of the Nepeña Valley (Engel 1957b: 74–75; Thompson 1964a: 206). However, testing in two low preceramic mounds, one near the center of the site and another against a hill toward the

Fig. 3. General view from the west of the Cotton Preceramic site of Huaynuná. Workmen are testing the midden, which is distinguishable on the surface as white patches of marine shell.

Fig. 4. View of small mound structure on a hillside at the west end of Huaynuná.

south (fig. 4), revealed that both were small platforms with stone masonry construction.

Artifacts

A small circle of worked gourd rind, a stick wrapped with cotton thread, and a shell fishhook (fig. 5a) are the only nontextile artifacts recovered at Huaynuná. The fishhook was fashioned from a valve of the large purple mussel *Choromytilus chorus*. The point is broken, but the shank is still bound with cotton cord that served as a line.

At Huaynuná, cotton was made into both twined textiles and looped netting. Since the netting is looped but not knotted, only large pieces retain their shape, and many of the isolated cords we encountered may well have once formed parts of nets. A significant portion of the artifacts at Huaynuná can be correlated with marine exploitation; fishing was accomplished both with hooks and lines and with nets.

Subsistence

Marine products comprise all of the faunal inventory, and most are from rocky areas. These include large quantities of the mussels *Semimytilus algosus, Brachidontes purpuratus,* and *Aulocomya ater,* the gastropod *Crepidula dilatata,* and barnacles, as well as moderately abundant remains of the mussel *Choromytilus chorus,* the gastropods *Tegula atra* and *Thais chocolata,* sea urchins and tunicates (*Piura chilensis*)—all of which occur in virtually every stratum of the controlled excavation. Remains of crab, chiton, limpets, and four gastropods (*Thais delessertiana, Cantharus* sp., *Concholepas concholepas,* and *Prunum curtum*) also occur consistently throughout the cut, but only in relatively small quantities. Of the sand-dwelling species, *Mesodesma donacium* is abundantly represented in the upper levels of the deposit, becoming more rare in lower levels, whereas *Argopecten purpuratum,* the scallop, occurs in moderate quantities throughout. The clam, *Mesodesma donacium,* was probably taken along the sandy beach, and *Choromytilus chorus* and the scallop, *Argopecten purpuratum,* from slightly deeper water. Discarded heads of small fish are also common; the fish were probably taken using nets or small hooks like the example made from mussel shell that we encountered during excavation.

Plant remains are well preserved and occurred in all the excavated

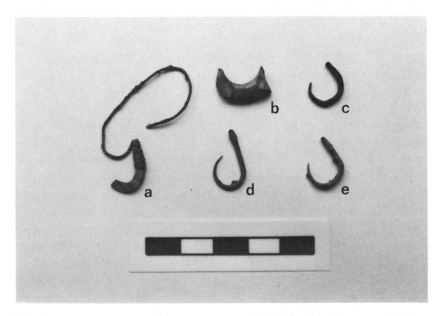

Fig. 5. Fishhooks from various sites: *a* is a shell fishhook with an attached cotton line from Huaynuná, *b* is a partial bone fishhook from Initial Period Las Haldas, *c* is a cactus-spine fishhook from Tortugas, and *d* and *e* are cactus-spine fishhooks from San Diego.

levels. Cotton (*Gossypium barbadense*) and gourd (*Lagenaria sicera-ria*) remains are most abundantly and consistently represented through-out the stratigraphic excavations. The excavated sample includes gourd seeds and rinds as well as cotton seeds, fibers, and boll and stem parts. Moderate amounts of squash (*Cucurbita ficifolia* and *C. maxima*) and *lúcuma* (*Lucuma bifera*) are fairly evenly distributed through the strata cut, whereas remains of pepper (*Capsicum* sp.), potatoes (*Solanum tuberosum*) (Ugent et al. 1982: 84–87, 1983: 4–7), sweet potatoes (*Ipomoea batatas*) (Ugent et al. 1981: 405, 1983: 3), *achira* (*Canna edulis*) (Ugent et al. 1984: 420), and unidentified bean pods occur more rarely within the middle levels of the excavation. Marine algae, cane (*Gynerium sagittatum*), and other wild plants were also recovered.

LAS HALDAS

Las Haldas, on the coast about 20 kilometers south of the Casma Valley (fig. 2), is the best known of the sites explored during this study. The site covers almost 40 hectares, most of which is midden. The central area (fig. 6) is dominated by a large mound and plaza structure measuring about 400 by 200 meters and flanked by several smaller but still sub-stantial mounds. Las Haldas lies against a small hill at an elevation of about 50 meters and about 100 meters from the ocean. Immediately adja-cent to the site, the drop to a rugged rocky beach is abrupt, but slightly farther north and south are more gradually sloping areas of sandy open beach.

Persons such as Lanning, Moseley, Kelley, and Engel, who are well ac-quainted with the nature of early coastal sites, have surveyed and occa-sionally tested Las Haldas. Fung, Grieder, and two Japanese expeditions made more substantial excavations. Working from this considerable data base, our excavations and reconnaissance were designed to more thor-oughly investigate problems of chronology and subsistence.

Las Haldas was discovered in 1957 by Engel and Lanning (Fung 1969: 13) and is described by Engel as a site with successive waves of pre-ceramic, pre-Chavin, and Chavin occupation, each associated with in-creasingly complex architecture (Engel 1963: 11, 1970: 32–33). On the basis of his fieldwork in the 1950s, Lanning considered Las Haldas to be an Initial Period temple or ceremonial center. He described the cere-monial complex as a series of temples with three plazas, including the plaza with the circular forecourt, all of which covered a small area

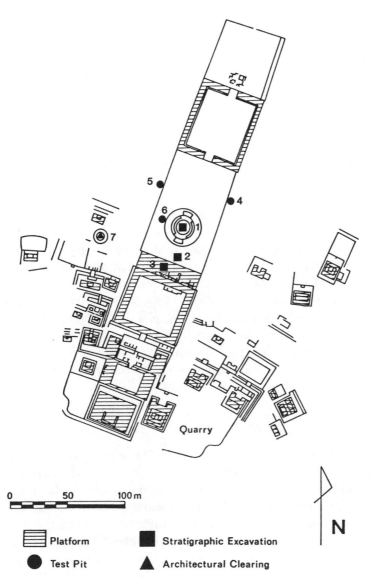

Fig. 6. Plan of the main temple and associated architecture of Las Haldas, showing locations of 1980 excavations.

compared to the earlier preceramic refuse (Lanning 1967: 91). Moseley concurs with this view, but treats Las Haldas as an anomaly because it is the only sizable Initial Period corporate-labor construction on the coast (Moseley 1975: 107).

Excavations at Las Haldas by Fung, Grieder, and the Tokyo expeditions of 1958 and 1969 have isolated four major occupation phases at the site (Fung 1969; Grieder 1975; Ishida et al. 1960: 194–197, 444–447; Matsuzawa 1978). These include a Cotton Preceramic component, a long period of early ceramic or Initial Period construction and midden deposition, the construction of the main mound complex, and a brief superficial Early Horizon occupation. The results of our fieldwork are in general agreement with this four-phase chronological framework.

Since previous investigators had already exposed areas suitable for stratigraphic excavations, we were able to extend our stratigraphic cuts off theirs. Cuts 1–3 (fig. 6) are three separate excavations designed to recover refuse from the Cotton Preceramic Period, the Initial Period, and the Early Horizon components respectively. We carried out four additional excavations. Cuts 4 and 5 are test pits that explored midden possibly associated with the main temple structure. Cut 6 investigated the relationship of the exterior of the sunken circular forecourt to surrounding midden deposits, and Cut 7 was a partial clearing of the small circular court at the site.

PRECERAMIC LAS HALDAS

The Cotton Preceramic component at Las Haldas is overlain by extensive early ceramic refuse and architecture which currently form the visible portion of the site. Previous investigators of Las Haldas penetrated preceramic midden at only three locations within the site. Rosa Fung, working with the Tokyo expedition in 1958, cut through the floor of the large circular forecourt and encountered about 2 meters of preceramic midden beneath a floorlike weathered surface which was overlain by ceramic levels (Fung 1969: fig. 8). Two pits excavated in 1967 by Grieder to the east of the main mound and plaza complex reached sterile and exposed preceramic refuse 2 meters or more below the surface (Grieder 1975). A profile of one cut reveals that the preceramic deposit was about 2 meters thick. Although the exact locations of his pits have not been described, Engel also tested at Las Haldas and has published a radiocarbon date of 1850 ± 80 B.C. for preceramic portions of the occupation (Engel 1966: 82).

The preceramic midden discovered by Fung and Grieder is as much as 120 meters apart, and two of the three documented exposures of preceramic midden are at least 2 meters thick. Thus, we are dealing with a substantial deposit covering a wide area, but probably not the areal extent realized by the subsequent ceramic occupation. Engel (1970: 32, 42) suggests that preceramic architecture is present at Las Haldas, but none of the detailed excavation reports corroborates this evidence.

In both areas Grieder excavated, the preceramic deposit was overlain by 2 meters or more of later ceramic-period debris. However, beneath the floor of the larger circle, the preceramic refuse was covered by as little as 90 centimeters of ceramic occupation. In order to obtain a sample of Las Haldas preceramic subsistence remains more rapidly, we elected to clean and work from an extant cut that had encountered preceramic refuse, and we specifically chose Fung's excavation beneath the sunken circle because there was less ceramic-period overburden (fig. 7). We excavated an 80-by-120-centimeter rectangle (fig. 6, Cut 1) of this midden by natural levels to sterile sand. We had hoped to sample a continuous midden sequence from the preceramic through the succeeding ceramic period, but ceramic levels beneath the floor of the circle had

Fig. 7. View from northeast of excavation of Cut 1 within the sunken circular forecourt of Las Haldas.

been badly disturbed and redistributed as fill during the construction of the sunken circle.

From charcoal recovered from our excavation into the preceramic component at Las Haldas, we were able to obtain three radiocarbon dates: 1795 ± 60 B.C. (UGA-4530), 1835 ± 60 B.C. (UGA-4529), and 2010 ± 80 B.C. (UGA-4531) (table 2). All three of these dates coincide well with the single preceramic date Engel obtained and fix the preceramic component of Las Haldas within the late Cotton Preceramic Period, contemporary with the occupation at Huaynuná.

Burial

In the process of excavating the preceramic strata, we encountered a child burial (fig. 8) 105 centimeters below the weathered surface which marks the upper boundary of the Cotton Preceramic refuse. The body was on its back in a flexed position, with the head toward the southwest. On the basis of bone size and absence of tooth eruption, we ascertained a skeletal age of less than six months. The body had been wrapped in one or more layers of twined cotton textile and subsequently in a single layer of *junco* (*Cyperus* sp.). Numerous large boulders had been placed over and around the body as the tomb was sealed.

Artifacts

In addition to the textiles associated with the burial, we encountered a very few additional fragments of badly decomposed twined textiles dur-

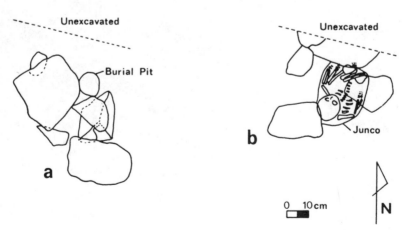

Fig. 8. Plan of the preceramic burial found within the midden of Cut 1 below the sunken circular forecourt of Las Haldas.

ing the excavations. These were the only artifacts recovered from the preceramic Las Haldas midden.

Subsistence

The Las Haldas preceramic midden, sampled by Cut 1, is quite sandy, and the component subsistence remains are not so dense as in ceramic middens. Shellfish are abundant, and the main species include the clam *Mesodesma donacium* from local sandy bays, as well as *Brachidontes purpuratus, Choromytilus chorus,* chiton, sea urchin, limpets, and tunicates from the rocky areas. Other rock-perching species, including *Aulocomya ater, Tegula atra,* and *Concholepas concholepas,* as well as barnacles and crabs, occur in moderate amounts, whereas the mussel *Semimytilus algosus* and the large clams *Protothaca thaca* and *Eurhomalea rufa* are consistently present but relatively rare. Remains of the land snail, *Scutalus* species, are abundant, and these animals were probably collected from *lomas* (fog vegetation) areas north of the site.

Plant remains are relatively rare, and much of the material we recovered is carbonized. Gourd rinds, cotton seeds and fiber, and wild *Tillandsia* sp. (the latter was used as fuel) are relatively abundant, but we also recovered marine algae and very rare and sporadic examples of guava (*Psidium guayaba*) and probably common beans and avocado (*Persea americana*).

EARLY INITIAL PERIOD LAS HALDAS

Directly overlying the compact, weathered surface of the Cotton Preceramic refuse are the remains of a long Initial Period phase of construction and midden deposition. The temple is built on this Initial Period deposit, and most of the outlying midden which surrounds the temple forms part of this pretemple occupation. Matsuzawa (1978: 666) published radiocarbon dates of 1650 ± 95 B.C., 1200 ± 90 B.C., and 640 ± 80 B.C. for this phase, and Grieder published a date of 1190 ± 80 B.C. for a similar ceramic context beneath the circular forecourt floor (Grieder 1975: 100, 106, 108–109). Matsuzawa (1978) questions the dates of 570 ± 60 B.C., 640 ± 80 B.C., and 410 ± 90 B.C. because all three are clearly too recent in view of other dates from the same contexts, and all were processed by the same laboratory. Although Grieder believed he was sampling ash on the floor of the circular forecourt, our excavations have revealed that the sample was from a hearth just above the compact, weathered surface of the preceramic deposit which Grieder mistook for a floor. The weathered floor of the sunken circle is over 90 centimeters above this surface, and the intervening deposit is pretemple Initial Period refuse. Grieder's second date of 1480 ± 80 B.C., which is from just outside the temple and within strata which exend beneath it, also serves to place this occupation chronologically (Grieder 1975: 99–100, pl. 40, fig. 5). Finally, we feel that the refuse his Cut 3 penetrated, east of the temple, is also part of this extensive occupation (Grieder 1975: 104).

Our test pits sampled this Initial Period midden at four points near and beneath the temple. Two of the cuts (fig. 6, Cuts 4 and 5) were made on either side and just outside of the plaza containing the circular forecourt. Two other cuts (Cuts 6 and 2) penetrated the surface of this plaza to expose stratified refuse just outside and west of the circle and near the stairway leading to the plaza immediately south. Our excavation (Cut 1), which cleaned the south face of the long trench Fung (1969: fig. 3) had excavated in the large circular forecourt, also exposed this Initial Period deposit. We had hoped to obtain a continuous sequence with the underlying preceramic midden, but it is evident from the profile (fig. 9) that the original excavation to construct the sunken circle had disturbed most of the Initial Period midden below it. Stratified midden is visible beneath and outside the architecture which forms the

Fig. 9. View from northeast of midden below and near the western edge of the inner wall of the sunken court at Las Haldas.

circle, whereas almost no stratification is present within this midden between the circular forecourt floor and the hard lens which caps the preceramic midden. The stratified midden is clearly truncated near the
western edge of the innermost face of the circle. After evaluating the
situation, we decided not to use this area for our Initial Period stratigraphic excavation. Because of the mixed deposition, there is also some
question as to the validity of Fung's (1969: 66–117) three ceramic phases,
which are based on her excavation of this area.

We selected a location near the stairway (fig. 6, Cut 2) for controlled
excavation by natural levels, and we accomplished the excavation by
cleaning the face of pit '58P1, which the Japanese had excavated (Matsuzawa 1978: 657, 659) and which exposed the early Initial Period architecture. We excavated a meter square area down to a floor, which
was encountered at a depth of 149 centimeters. It is certain that the Initial Period deposit is much deeper at this locus, but factors of time and
the small size of the excavation unit made it advisable to stop at such a
convenient cultural feature as this floor. We obtained three radiocarbon
dates from charcoal from this cut: 1190 ± 75 B.C. (UGA-4533), 1510 ± 75
B.C. (UGA-4532), and 1645 ± 75 B.C. (UGA-4534) (table 2). These dates
agree with those of Grieder and the earlier ones of Matsuzawa, placing
this deposit well within the Initial Period.

Architecture

Several pits by previous excavators encountered architecture associated
with the pretemple refuse. This architecture consists of small domestic
structures of double-faced cobble walls with rubble fill (Grieder 1975;
Matsuzawa 1978). Such structures are present both buried beneath subsequent temple architecture and exposed on the surface in outlying
zones unaffected by monumental construction at the site. Floors are
finished with a coat of silt and fine sand 2 to 3 centimeters deep. These
structures vary in orientation, and they clearly predate and are not associated with subsequent temple construction at the site.

Artifacts

Ceramic fragments are the most common artifacts found in the ceramic
levels at Las Haldas. In the pretemple Initial Period refuse, the main vessel forms are neckless ollas, jars, and bottles. Principal types of decoration on vessel exteriors include incision, punctation, and zoned punctation. There are also several sherds with textile and net impressions on

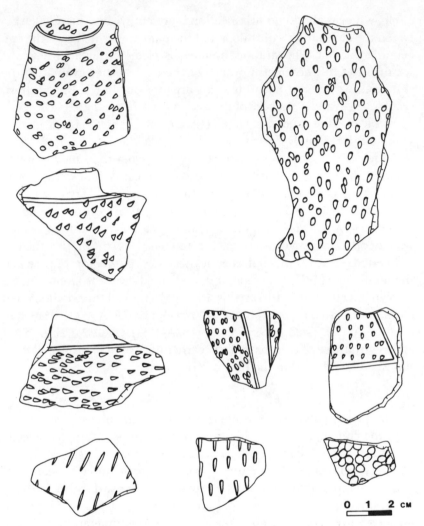

Fig. 10. Excavated ceramics found within Initial Period midden at Las Haldas. Incision and punctation are present on sherd exteriors.

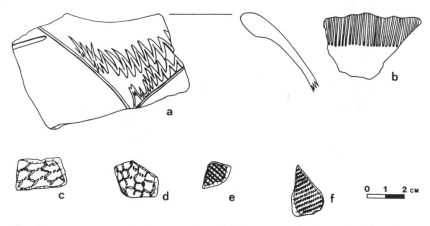

Fig. 11. Excavated ceramics from Las Haldas: *a* and *b* are from the Early Horizon deposit and illustrate the decorative techniques of rocker-stamping and combing, respectively; *c–f* are from the Initial Period refuse and illustrate techniques of net impression (*c, d*) and textile impression made on the interior surfaces of vessels (*e, f*).

the interior surfaces (figs. 10 and 11c–f). A few zoned red slip and zoned black graphite sherds we found correlate with ceramics in the upper levels of cuts made by Grieder (1975: 105, 112). Ceramics recovered from pretemple refuse correspond well with examples excavated by Fung (1969) and Grieder (1975), not only in terms of decoration but also form. Specifically, our 1980 excavations recovered neckless olla rims (round, bevelled, and fold-under varieties) similar to those of Grieder (1975: fig. 11) and Fung (1969: figs. 12a–b, 13a–j, 14a–l, 15a–m, 16a–m, and 19a–p). The few narrow-necked bottles or jars we recovered resemble those of Grieder (1975: fig. 11) and Fung (1969: fig. 17b–c, e–i).

Nonceramic artifacts recovered from the early Initial Period refuse at Las Haldas include a bone fishhook (fig. 5b), a cut bird-bone tube, and part of a grinding stone. There are also textiles, including short lengths of *junco* cord and vegetable-fiber looped netting, as well as cotton knotted netting and numerous cotton textiles, all of which are woven. We also recovered a piece of what may be a cotton sling.

We recovered a fragmentary stone vessel bottom from the surface some 70 meters south of the main temple. Fung (1969: 28–29) encountered two stone bowl fragments on the surface of Las Haldas as well. What early time period these fragments belong to is unknown, but they closely resemble examples found at Pampa de las Llamas-Moxeke and are therefore mentioned here along with early Initial Period artifacts from Las Haldas.

Subsistence

Preliminary evidence indicates that virtually all animal remains from this early Initial Period occupation of Las Haldas came from the nearby ocean. The major exception consists of abundant remains of land snails which were plentiful in the *lomas* areas a few kilometers north of the site on Cerro Las Lomas. The abundance of gastropod and mussel species such as *Tegula atra, Turbo niger, Semimytilus algosus, Choromytilus chorus, Brachidontes purpuratus, Aulocomya ater*, limpets, and chiton, as well as crabs, sea urchins, and tunicates, reveals that much exploitation focused on rocky littoral zones. Barnacles and *Crepidula dilatata*, which occurred in moderate amounts, and *Thais chocolata, Thais delessertiana*, and *Concholepas concholepas*, which were consistently present but relatively rare, are also rock-dwelling species. However, *Mesodesma donacium* remains were abundant, and *Eurhomalea rufa* and *Protothaca thaca* occurred in moderate quantities, indicating that clams were also harvested from the sandy beaches. At Las Haldas, the individual shells which form the debris from the consumption of shellfish are unusually large—much larger than modern examples from the same locality. It would seem that during the Initial Period the site's inhabitants were collecting from old shellfish beds which were not yet showing the effects of intensive exploitation. We also recovered bones of fish, birds, whales, and especially sea lions from this midden.

Plant remains within the Initial Period midden are better preserved than preceramic examples, and quite varied. Cotton seeds and fiber, gourd rind fragments and seeds, and *lúcuma* seed parts are most abundant. Common beans (*Phaseolus vulgaris*) and peanuts (*Arachis hypogaea*) occur in moderate amounts, whereas remains of potatoes (Ugent et al. 1982: 188–189, 1983: 9–10) are relatively rare. Peppers (*Capsicum* sp.), lima beans (*Phaseolus lunatus*), *pacae* (*Inga feuillei*), and *cansaboca* (*Bunchosia armeniaca*) also occur rarely and sporadically. We have also identified algae and wild plant species such as *Tillandsia*.

LAS HALDAS INITIAL PERIOD MOUND COMPLEX

The Initial Period mound complex, which is the main surface feature of Las Haldas, was constructed during the third occupational phase defined at the site. This involved the building of the main mound with its long series of plazas, as well as the construction of numerous adjacent smaller mound and platform complexes. The two sunken circular forecourts form part of this temple complex. Although we recognize the construction of the temple as an important event in the development of the site, during our fieldwork at Las Haldas we were unable to locate refuse which was unequivocally associated with the main mound construction and use. This, plus other data, have led us to conclude that this phase was quite brief, yet very visible. During our examination of the Las Haldas temple complex we made many additional observations concerning its construction and use.

The builders of Las Haldas took advantage of the local hill toward the south to increase the apparent height of the structure while investing less labor. On parts of this hill, especially in southern areas where there was no earlier Initial Period midden, fill of angular stones loosely encased in reed bags was employed in the temple construction. Samples from such bags below the main staircase yielded radiocarbon dates of 1530 ± 130 B.C. and 570 ± 60 B.C. (Matsuzawa 1978). Farther north, where earlier midden was quite deep, the ashy matrix was scraped up to form a base for the mound and platforms. This is especially evident immediately east and west of the main mound plazas, where this practice has left clear troughs between the temple structure and the nearest outlying refuse. Beneath the central portion of the temple and plazas, earlier Initial Period midden was virtually undisturbed, as exemplified by the deposit near the main staircase we selected for a controlled stratigraphic excavation (fig. 6, Cut 2). After the mounds and plazas were formed, the temple surface was finished with a yellow layer which was probably a plaster of fine sand and silt applied to conceal the dark, ashy midden. Although it is weathered to a fine powder, this surface finish is still readily visible over most of the monumental architecture at the site.

Our excavations and the excavation data of Grieder (1975) and the Japanese team (Matsuzawa 1978) document the existence of two phases of temple construction at Las Haldas. In 1969, the Japanese exposed a set of stairs behind the main staircase which may have afforded access to an earlier temple construction (Matsuzawa 1978: 659, 664). Grieder (1975) has made a distinction between an earlier phase characterized by yellow-to-tan mortar and plaster and a brief later phase marked by the use of a gray-white granular finishing material he describes as "concrete mortar." He located "concrete" on walls and a floor of the main mound and asserts, on the basis of surveying tools still in place, that this phase was left unfinished (Grieder 1975: 102–103). Analysis of this "concrete" shows that it is primarily made of crushed seashells mixed with sand and has a very high salt content, probably derived from seawater used for mixing (George Harlow, personal communication; Edmund Dlutow-ski, personal communication).

We have observed this "concrete" in other contexts, most notably lining the larger circular forecourt. This, plus additional evidence, suggests that the circular court is a late feature excavated into a completed temple construction. During our attempts to locate refuse clearly associated with the use of the temple, we immediately noticed a large volume of midden mounded against the east sidewall of the plaza containing the large circular court. Testing of this ashy refuse (fig. 6, Cut 4) revealed a lack of internal stratigraphy; this is characteristic of redeposited material. At the bottom of the disturbed deposit near the base of the plaza wall we found nodules of the yellow silty sand used to cap the mound and plaza surfaces. These two features led us to conclude that we were dealing with backdirt from the circle which had been cut into a plaza already finished with yellow plaster.

The floor of this circle is finished with 5 centimeters of yellow-white silt which is clearly visible near the circumference, where it is preserved beneath rocks fallen from the lining. Both Fung (1969: 60) and Matsuzawa (1978: 662) have asserted that there is no prepared floor in this circle. Instead, they state that the yellow layer is silt washed in from the forecourt walls by occasional rains. Part of the yellow layer is deposited sediment, but not all. Grieder (1975: 100), as previously noted, misidentified the hard layer separating preceramic from ceramic midden as the forecourt floor.

The smaller circular court associated with one or more small mounds west of the main complex is not necessarily contemporaneous with the large circular court. Partly exposed by Cut 7 (fig. 6), the smaller circular court is not lined with the "concrete" mortar that the large circle is, but rather with the earlier tan, silty clay mortar noted by Grieder (1975). This fact, plus the circle's association with mounds that have orientations slightly askew from the main temple complex, could indicate that this circle and its associated mounds slightly predate the large circle and perhaps are associated with an earlier phase of main temple construction.

EARLY HORIZON LAS HALDAS

The final early ceramic occupation documented for the site of Las Haldas is associated with the disuse of the main mound complex. Grieder (1975: 103) characterizes the structures as the "work of impoverished survivors occupying a famous ruin" because the walls are but one stone deep and irregularly laid out, much like windscreens. They occupy the mound and plaza surfaces, especially where the monumental architecture offers protection from the wind, as well as outlying areas. On the temple, the very ashy refuse associated with this occupation buries much of the main staircase and overlies other mound architectural features in occasional concentrated patches. Radiocarbon dates of 880 ± 70 B.C., 780 ± 70 B.C. (Grieder 1975: 100, 109), 730 ± 150 B.C., and 410 ± 90 B.C. (Matsuzawa 1978: 666) for midden overlying the main staircase are in agreement with the late appearance of the squatterlike remains.

Our stratigraphic excavation into this late refuse (fig. 6, Cut 3) was a 1-by-1-meter extension off a trench the Japanese expedition had made in 1969 (Matsuzawa 1978: 657, fig. 4). We obtained three radiocarbon dates from charcoal collected from this cut: 895 ± 80 B.C. (UGA-4528), 965 ± 60 B.C. (UGA-4527), and 1040 ± 75 B.C. (UGA-4526) (table 2). These dates are slightly earlier than, but within acceptable confidence limits of, the three oldest previously reported dates from this context.

Artifacts

In the posttemple refuse, we encountered very few sherds. The few ceramics found by Fung (1969) in this deposit are similar to our specimens. The neckless olla is the predominant form (see Fung 1969: fig. 23d–g), and combing and rocker-stamping (fig. 11a–b) are present in addition to incision and punctation as forms of decoration.

The very few nonceramic artifacts within this posttemple deposit can be correlated with the marine focus of the occupation. These include a grooved stone net sinker as well as fragments of both knotted and looped cotton netting.

Subsistence

Although the species are marine, faunal remains from the Cut 3 sample of posttemple occupation of Las Haldas differ considerably from inventories documented for earlier middens. Chiton plates and sea urchin test fragments and spines are extremely abundant, often occurring as thick bands of remains where these are the dominant species. There is correspondingly less variety among the other species regularly used. Thus, shellfish procurement focused on a single rocky habitat and a small range of species. All other significant species reflect this exploitation pattern. These include moderate amounts of *Brachidontes purpuratus*, *Crepidula dilatata*, *Tegula atra*, limpets, tunicates, and barnacles, as well as relatively rare occurrences of *Semimytilus algosus, Aulocomya ater*, and crab remains, all of which are rock-dwelling species.

The only plant which occurs abundantly in this deposit is marine algae. Large stalks occur too frequently to have been accidentally brought to the site as a by-product of marine collecting, and the carbonized state of many such stalks has led Fung (personal communication) to suggest that they were used as fuel. All other remains of plants are moderately abundant to rare, but a considerable variety of domesticates is present. This includes moderate amounts of gourd rinds, cotton seeds and fiber, peanut, and maize (*Zea mays*), which first occurs at Las Haldas in this Early Horizon component. These maize remains are concentrated in the middle and lower levels of this stratigraphic excavation. Additionally, common beans, *lúcuma*, and pepper remains as well as tuber species of manioc (*Manihot esculentum*) (Ugent et al. 1985: 92) and *achira* (Ugent et al. 1984: 422–423) occur consistently but relatively rarely within Cut 3. We have also identified *Canavalia* beans, avocado seeds, and squash remains from this context, but they are rare and their occurrence is intermittent.

PAMPA DE LAS LLAMAS-MOXEKE

The site of Pampa de las Llamas-Moxeke is located in a large, flat quebrada on the Casma branch of the Casma Valley, about 18 kilometers from the Pacific Ocean (fig. 2). It is about 150 meters above sea level. It was first explored in the late nineteenth century by Middendorf (1973a: 219–223), who described the Moxeke mound proper and parts of Pampa de las Llamas. Middendorf (1973a: 219–220) relates that the name Pampa de las Llamas comes from a local legend which says that five hundred llamas laden with treasure for Atahualpa's ransom were sacrificed there and the treasure buried when word came that Atahualpa had been killed. In 1937, Tello (1956: 44–46) made a more detailed study and published a plan of the site (Tello 1956: fig. 2, opposite p. 32) which is fairly accurate, especially considering that it was executed using only a compass and a tape measure (Donald Collier, personal communication). Though Tello originally described the area as a single site and some investigators have followed suit (Sanders and Marino 1970: 71–72), other authors separate Pampa de las Llamas and Moxeke into two or more sites (Collier, 1962: 412; Thompson 1962a: 294–297), whereas others mention only the Moxeke mound proper (Kauffmann 1980: 275–278; Lumbreras 1974: 68; Roe 1974: 33–34; Willey 1971: 123). We feel, however, on the basis of proximity, architectural similarities, alignment, and artifactual evidence, that Pampa de las Llamas and Moxeke must be considered as a single site.

Tello (1956: 44–46) was the first archaeologist to suggest that Pampa de las Llamas-Moxeke dated to Chavin times or the Early Horizon. Both Collier (1962: 44) and Thompson (1961: 71, 191–192, 1962a: 294, 1964a: 207) date Moxeke to the Middle Formative, 750 to 400 B.C., whereas Thompson (1961: 96–97, 187–191, 1962a: 297) dates the main mound at Pampa de las Llamas to the Late Formative, 400 to 0 B.C./A.D. Rosa Fung (1972: 9), on the other hand, dates the main occupation of the Pampa de las Llamas mound to the Initial Period.

In order to resolve the chronological placement of the site as well as investigate its subsistence base, in 1980 we placed forty-three test pits measuring approximately 1 by 1 meter in various midden areas to determine which areas would be best for detailed stratigraphic excavations. We expanded and excavated six of these test pits by natural levels (fig. 12). Cuts 1–4 were single 1-meter squares, whereas Cut 5 consisted of

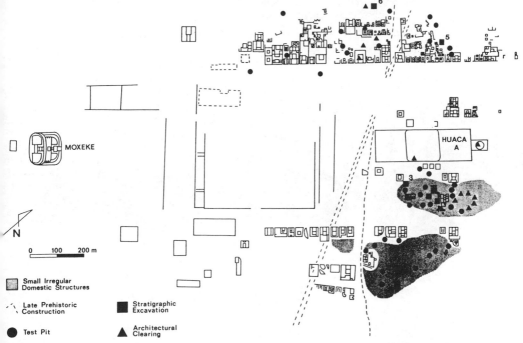

Fig. 12. Plan of the Initial Period site of Pampa de las Llamas-Moxeke, showing locations of 1980 excavations. The site is dominated by two large mounds, Huaca A and Moxeke.

three contiguous 1-meter squares and Cut 6 of two contiguous 1-meter squares. We made fourteen additional cuts to examine architecture at the site. Table 2 lists nine radiocarbon dates obtained from charcoal collected during the stratigraphic excavations in middens. With the exception of one date (2705 ± 95 B.C.) which is definitely too old, all of the dates place Pampa de las Llamas-Moxeke well within the Initial Period. The average date for the site is about 1400 B.C., and its occupation is clearly contemporary with the Initial Period occupation at Las Haldas.

Architecture

We executed the plan of Pampa de las Llamas-Moxeke (fig. 12) using a combination of theodolite mapping, aerial photographs, excavation, and ground survey. The plan includes all early monumental and intermediate-sized architecture and has shaded areas indicating the areal extent of smaller irregular domestic dwellings. The southern third of the site rests within modern cultivation which has obscured much of the early architecture.

Dominating the site, which covers over 2 square kilometers, are two large mounds, Moxeke and Huaca A of Pampa de las Llamas. Both share a common magnetic orientation of N41°E. Moxeke (fig. 13) measures approximately 160 meters by 170 meters and stands about 30 me-

Fig. 13. General view of Moxeke from the north.

Fig. 14. General view from the southwest of Huaca A and surrounding architecture of Pampa de las Llamas-Moxeke.

ters high (Tello 1956: 57, fig. 25). It is basically rectangular in shape, with rounded corners, and has several terrace levels. On the third terrace level along the front, Tello (1956: 54–66) uncovered a number of large anthropomorphic sculptured friezes. Both stone and conical adobes were used in the construction of Moxeke, and the sculptured friezes are closely associated with the adobe portions of the mound.

Aligned with and facing Moxeke near the opposite end of the site is Huaca A (fig. 14). Tello (1956: 52, fig. 24) published a schematic plan of this mound. Huaca A measures about 135 meters by 120 meters, is about 12 meters high, and is slightly rhomboid in shape. Survey and excavation show that the mound is made principally of stone set in silty clay mortar with occasional use of conical adobes. The stone used was both quarried from nearby hills to the west and north and gathered from the surrounding quebrada surface.

Huaca A has two centrally placed entrances that lead to its summit, one on its southwest face and a second on its northeast face. The summit has a very regular and distinctive layout, which Thompson (1962a: 295) classified as a corridor subtype. Along the central axis of the summit is a series of five interconnected courts. At a higher level on each side of the central courtyard area is an identical arrangement of rooms: five pairs of large rooms alternate with six sets of narrow rooms. To the outside of these rooms along the northwest and southeast edges of the mound are two rows of eleven small rooms.

It appears that Huaca A may have had a more secular function than Moxeke and most other early coastal mounds because of the presence of so many rooms and their unusual patterned layout. This assessment of Huaca A is based on the contrast between its summit configuration and the more normal U-shaped configuration of most early mounds on the Peruvian coast, including Moxeke, which are generally considered to have had a religious function. Such mounds have associated plazas, including areas between the wings of their U, from which various segments of the site population observed public ceremonies (T. Pozorski 1980). On the other hand, the plazas directly associated with Huaca A are smaller, and the largest room, at the center of the mound, is relatively inaccessible. Finally, the small size and regularity of the peripheral rooms suggest that some of them may have had a storage function.

Huaca A is unique in the Casma Valley in that it has a large plaza at each end of its main axis. The plaza to the southwest faces Moxeke and measures 125 meters southeast-northwest by 110 meters northeast-southwest. It is excavated approximately 2 meters into the natural quebrada surface. The three sides of the plaza except the mound face are currently unlined and consist of mounded earth embankments against the natural quebrada deposition. However, it appears that the facing stones were robbed from the plaza to construct a late prehistoric wall and road which cross the site near the southwest end of the plaza. More than half of the plaza contains a substantial silt deposition up to 30 centimeters deep that is the result of occasional El Niño flood waters being trapped and evaporating within the plaza area. This is the area that has sometimes been referred to as a "reservoir" (Middendorf 1973a: 223; Tello 1956: 51–52).

The plaza off the northeast face of Huaca A is the same size as the southwest plaza and is also excavated into the natural quebrada deposits. However, the plaza sides are lined with two and, on the southeast side, three rows of boulders forming steplike small terraces. Much of the northern half of the plaza has been eroded by runoff water from occasional past rains. In particular, a portion of the northeast side and the west corner of the plaza have been completely washed away.

Off the northeast side of the northern plaza is a raised platform measuring 40 meters wide, 60 meters long, and ranging from 3 meters high next to the plaza to only 30 centimeters high at its northeast end. Within the platform are the eroded remains of a sunken circular court, a common feature in early mound sites along the Peruvian coast. Found during our survey, this feature was unnoticed by previous investigators, probably because of its eroded condition. Only the southern one-third of the sunken court is well preserved: most of the remainder has been washed away by occasional floods. There are some boulder lines along the north and west parts of the circle, however, that permit a reasonably accurate reconstruction of the circle. The basic inner diameter of the circle is about 32 meters, but along the northeast-southwest axis the diameter is 39 meters because of the jogged wall configurations on the northeast and southwest sides of the circle. There are no staircases leading into the circle, but access could be easily gained anywhere along the northern half of the circle's perimeter.

Excavation into the preserved southern portion of the circular court (fig. 15) revealed the outer wall to be 72 centimeters high and associated with an original bench 1.55 meters wide and 12 centimeters high. Two

Fig. 15. Looking southwest at preserved southern portion of the circular fore-court of Huaca A.

later floors with gravel fill raised the bench surface an additional 22 centimeters and 11 centimeters respectively. Surface evidence in a washed-over portion of the circle to the west suggests multiple construction phases there as well.

The remaining architecture at Pampa de las Llamas-Moxeke consists of (1) over seventy small mound structures and a few walled enclosures ranging from 10 meters to over 50 meters on a side and 2 meters to 5 meters high, and (2) several hundred small single- and multi-room domestic structures (fig. 16). The majority of the small mounds are arranged in two long rows near the eastern and western edges of the site. The small mounds are made of quarried stone and locally deposited quebrada boulders set in silty clay mortar. They generally align with the natural drainage pattern of the quebrada which runs northeast to southwest, and erosion has enhanced their heights. Nevertheless, a substantial amount of excavation and artificial mounding characterizes their construction.

The rows of small mounds are precisely aligned with the orientation of both the Moxeke mound and Huaca A of Pampa de las Llamas and demarcate the sides of four or five enormous plazas between the two mounds. Most of the two rows of mounds are currently outside of cultivation and hence are well preserved, but one can see isolated small mounds and walls continuing into the cultivated zone. These mounds come to within 200 meters of Moxeke. The remaining small mound structures form numerous shorter rows parallel to both the two long rows of mounds and the two main mounds of the site. Some of the mounds and enclosures, particularly near Huaca A, give the distinct impression of being unfinished. Several areas have mounded earth or excavated pits associated with unused piles of stones presumably intended for use as facing. An overall view of the layout of the numerous small mounds and enclosures suggests that the two long rows were initially laid out along with the Moxeke mound and Huaca A and were followed by continuous construction of adjacent parallel rows of mounds, some of which were not completed when the site was abandoned.

The domestic structures are concentrated in two main areas: (1) in a large area to the east of Huaca A and its two associated plazas and (2) along the western edge of the site just outside of the western row of small mounds. The domestic area east of Huaca A is especially well preserved and is associated with abundant midden deposits up to 1.5 meters deep. On the other hand, portions of the western domestic area, which is also associated with midden deposits, have been adversely affected by

Fig. 16. View of a partially excavated domestic structure east of Huaca A, Pampa de las Llamas-Moxeke.

occasional runoff water from adjacent hillsides. There is some indication that a substantial domestic component existed between Huaca A and the western row of small mounds, but most of this has been washed away by runoff within the most active channel of the quebrada drainage pattern.

Individual rooms of domestic structures are usually square to rectangular, with walls ranging from 2 to 5 meters in length. Walls are usually of double-faced wet-laid stone construction with rubble-filled cores (fig. 16). The walls generally stand only one to three stones high, resulting in 60-centimeter maximum height, and there is little evidence to suggest that the stone construction stood much higher. There is evidence of postholes, however, in corners that probably contained wooden or cane supports for perishable superstructures. Excavations showed most floors to be covered by only 5 to 30 centimeters of fallen debris, with some floors lying exposed on the surface, affected only by wetting from occasional rains. Most of the domestic structures cleared have floors that are level with the surrounding terrain, but some are artificially raised, and one in particular has a stepped entrance. Limited excavations uncovered small rectangular and circular hearths within some structures, but there is evidence in the form of burned rock and charcoal concentrations to suggest that some cooking was done outside structures as well.

Much of the central and eastern portions of the site are crossed by later linear features, such as roads and canals, that affect portions of the earlier architecture (fig. 12). At least four roads are present—two irregular ones running north to south and two straight roads running southeast to northwest. The longer of the straight roads, which Tello (1956: 51–53, fig. 2, opposite p. 32) describes as a *"camino inkaico,"* runs from the side of Cerro San Francisco along the western edge of the site toward the site of El Purgatorio, which primarily contains later Casma Incised pottery. One long late prehistoric wall crosses the entire site just south of the Huaca A complex. Both modern and late prehistoric canals that originate to the east of the site cross the large plazas between Moxeke and Huaca A. Some of these canals follow paths originally delineated by low plaza-wall divisions. Associated with the canals are remnants of serpentine furrow fields.

Finally, in the southeast corner of the site, west of Moxeke, there are a number of late prehistoric structures (some are not included in fig. 12) associated with Casma Incised and Chimu pottery. These include the structures around Tello's "Plaza I" (Tello 1956: 49–50, fig. 2, opposite p. 32) as well as a large structure with numerous regularly spaced rooms that Thompson (1961: 121, 125, 282–284, 1964b: 97–99) dates as Chimu and Inca.

Artifacts

Pottery sherds constitute the most common type of artifacts found at Pampa de las Llamas-Moxeke. The range of vessel forms is somewhat limited. Neckless ollas are the most common form, with some occurrence of bowls, jars, and bottles (figs. 17 and 18). We also encountered fragments of solid figurines and spindle whorls. Ceramic decoration, like vessel form, is quite limited. The most common decorative technique is punctation, which usually occurs as large and deep angular punctations arranged in a line along the angled shoulder or on modeled protrusions of the body of neckless ollas (fig. 17). At times these punctations were burnished over after they had been made. This type of decoration is exactly like that described and illustrated by Fung (1972: 5, fig. 1, lámina 2) from her survey of the site in 1968. In addition to the large punctations, our ceramic sample also includes small punctations, zoned punctation, incision, incised appliqué bumps, modeling, and incised raised

Fig. 17. Neckless olla rims from Pampa de las Llamas-Moxeke, with large punctations and incised lines decorating the angled shoulder of each vessel.

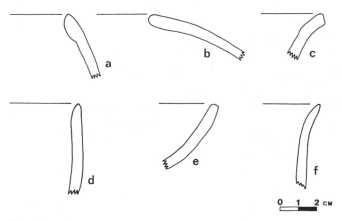

Fig. 18. Rim profiles of ceramic vessels from Pampa de las Llamas-Moxeke, including neckless ollas (*a*, *b*), a jar (*c*), bowls (*d*, *e*), and a bottle (*f*).

Fig. 19. Stone bowl rim, bottom, and body fragments collected from the western edge of Pampa de las Llamas-Moxeke. The exterior of the rim in the center of the top row has an incised face design.

bands. The interiors of most sherds are well smoothed, and few exhibit the streaky interior wiping marks that are common on pottery from many early coastal sites.

A second important type of artifact encountered at Pampa de las Llamas-Moxeke is the polished flat-bottomed stone vessel (T. Pozorski and S. Pozorski, in press a). We have found several dozen fragments of polished stone vessels, including several rims, covers, and flat bottoms (fig. 19). Rim fragments indicate diameters ranging from 15 to 27 centimeters; the vessels are fairly tall (over 10 centimeters) and steep-sided. Bottoms are thick, measuring from 2 to almost 7 centimeters. Most rims have a slight exterior bulge that extends to about 1 centimeter below the lip. One rim (fig. 19) has an incised decoration on its exterior that is part of a face.

We found the stone vessel fragments on the surface and within excavated rooms and middens on both the western and eastern sides of the site. The presence of a few cover fragments and the lack of significant grinding evidence on several vessel bottoms indicate that some of the vessels were used as bowls or containers. However, it is also likely that many, if not most, of the vessels were actually used as mortars for grinding red pigment because some stone pestle fragments have been found in association with vessel fragments, and there is red pigment on the interior surfaces of many vessel bottoms. The red pigment ground on these mortars may have been used for decorating architecture, since both Middendorf (1973a: 220) and Tello (1956: 60–66) encountered much red pigment on the walls of Moxeke.

Tello (1956: 52) found two stone "mortar" fragments at Pampa de las Llamas-Moxeke, one of them reputedly decorated with incised figures; however, he found these fragments to the north of the main site at the foot of Cerro Pan de Azucar. Although stone bowls or mortars have been reported from several areas of Peru (Kauffmann 1980: 279–286; Lathrap 1970: 108, pls. 25–27), the examples which most closely resemble the Pampa de las Llamas-Moxeke collection are bowl rims from Huaca Negra in Viru (Strong and Evans 1952: 40–45) and from Caballo Muerto in the Moche Valley (T. Pozorski 1976), and two complete stone vessels, one from a grave at Punkurí in the Nepeña Valley and one from Huaca Suchiman in the Santa Valley (Tello 1943: 137). Stone bowl or mortar fragments which somewhat resemble the examples from Pampa de las Llamas-Moxeke have been found at Chavin de Huantar (Tello 1960: 302–304), but there is little evidence to indicate that these date as early as coastal examples.

We found both twined and woven textiles at Pampa de las Llamas-Moxeke (fig. 20); they are the best preserved examples known from an inland Initial Period site. Other Initial Period sites along the coast contain both twined and woven textiles (Conklin 1974; Lanning 1967: 80,

Fig. 20. Detail of twined textile found at Pampa de las Llamas-Moxeke.

111; S. Pozorski and T. Pozorski 1979a: 421; Willey 1971: 107), and this, along with the radiocarbon assays, helps confirm the dating of Pampa de las Llamas-Moxeke.

Other artifacts of note from the site include two projectile points, a hammerstone, and numerous shell paint palettes. The two projectile points (fig. 21) are made of local cherty siltstone. The upper one in figure 21, which we found on the surface near the center of the western edge of the site, has fine retouched edges. The lower point in figure 21, which we found approximately 30 centimeters below the surface in Cut 5, along the northwest edge of the site, has the same rounded stem but lacks the retouched edges of the other point. This lower darker point resembles an undated point from Huampucoto in the upper Sechin branch of the Casma Valley (Fung and Williams 1977: 146, pl. 6). Neither of the Pampa de las Llamas-Moxeke points, however, resembles examples dating to the early Preceramic Period in the Casma area (Malpass 1983: 1–14), nor are they directly comparable to points assigned to early ceramic periods in other areas of Peru (see, for example, MacNeish et al. 1980: 42, 78–94). Although in the context of Pampa de las Llamas-Moxeke the points stand out in an otherwise poorly developed lithic industry, they appear to be contemporary with the main site occupation and were probably used in hunting the deer which formed a significant

Fig. 21. Two stone projectile points found along the western edge of Pampa de las Llamas-Moxeke.

Fig. 22. Shells found at Pampa de las Llamas-Moxeke that were used as palettes to hold red pigment.

portion of the diet at this inland site. The other artifacts, a hammerstone and several large valves of the clams *Protothaca thaca* and *Eurhomalea rufa* (fig. 22), bear evidence of red pigment, which indicates that they are probably also connected with its processing or use.

Subsistence

Despite the inland location of Pampa de las Llamas-Moxeke relative to other sites of this study, most of the animal remains consumed at Pampa de las Llamas-Moxeke were marine in origin. Two rock-perching small mussel species, *Semimytilus algosus* and *Brachidontes purpuratus*, were abundantly represented within all stratigraphic excavations, occurring relatively uniformly throughout each deposit. We identified many other species, and these had a relatively consistent distribution throughout the levels of each stratigraphic cut unless otherwise indicated. Valves of the large mussels *Choromytilus chorus* and *Aulocomya ater*, as well as sea urchin tests, were abundant within Cut 4. *Choromytilus chorus* remains were moderate in frequency in all the remaining cuts, whereas *Aulocomya ater* was moderately abundant in Cuts 2 and 5 and relatively rare in Cuts 1, 3, and 6, occurring only in the upper part of Cut 1. Fragments of sea urchin tests were only moderately abundant in Cut 2 and relatively rare in Cut 1. Barnacles occurred in moderate amounts in all six cuts, and chiton plates were moderately abundant in all but Cut 6, where they were abundant, and Cut 5, where they were relatively rare. Among the remaining rock-perching species, limpets were relatively rare in all stratigraphic contexts except Cut 4 and were restricted to the upper levels of Cut 2; the gastropod *Crepidula dilatata* was moderately represented in Cut 5 remains but rare in Cuts 1, 4, and 6; and *Tegula atra*, another gastropod, occurred relatively rarely in Cut 2. Crab remains were moderately abundant in Cuts 5 and 6 and relatively rare in Cuts 2 and 3.

Although fewer of the significant species were sand-dwelling bivalves, several were of considerable importance. *Mesodesma donacium* remains were moderate in frequency in all cuts except Cut 6; *Eurhomalea rufa* remains were moderately represented in Cuts 1, 2, and 6; *Protothaca thaca* was present in moderate amounts in Cuts 2 (upper levels only), 5, and 6; and *Donax peruvianus* valves occurred relatively rarely in Cuts 3, 5, and 6. The shells of *Eurhomalea rufa* and the valves of *Protothaca thaca* were so frequently encrusted with red pigment that they may have been prized more as paint palettes or containers than food. Finally, the land snail, *Scutalus* sp., varied considerably in frequency, occurring abundantly in Cuts 1 (lower levels) and 2, in moderate amounts in Cuts 3 and 6, and relatively rarely in Cut 5. These frequencies suggest that this snail was also consumed at the site. Remains of fish, both dried heads and portions of dried meat, are also common at Pampa de las Llamas-Moxeke. These individual fish are quite small and were probably captured using nets or small hooks.

At Pampa de las Llamas-Moxeke we find the first evidence of land animals as a potential food source. A single fox or dog bone may be from an animal that was eaten, but remains of deer (*Odocoilius virginianus*) more definitely point to this large animal as a significant source of food.

Preservation is excellent at Pampa de las Llamas-Moxeke, and plant remains are abundant and in good condition. The significant plant species discussed here are consistently represented throughout the natural levels of each stratigraphic excavation unless otherwise indicated. Abundant species are almost always present in all levels, whereas relatively rare plants may have a more intermittent vertical distribution while still occurring in some upper, middle, and lower levels.

Cotton remains (fig. 23) in the form of seeds, fiber, and bolls are especially abundant in all six cuts, and peanut shell fragments also occur in

Fig. 23. Remains of cotton fiber and plant parts found in middens of Pampa de las Llamas-Moxeke.

high frequencies within all six stratigraphic contexts. Gourd seeds and rinds are abundant in Cuts 1–3, 5, and 6, and moderately represented in Cut 4. Remains of one squash (*Cucurbita maxima*) occur frequently in Cuts 1–3 and 6 and in moderate amounts in Cuts 4 and 5, and *lúcuma* is also either abundant (Cuts 2, 3, 5, and 6) or moderately abundant (Cuts 1 and 4). Tubers, including potatoes (Ugent et al. 1982: 183–185, 1983: 4–5), sweet potatoes (Ugent et al. 1981: 403–405, 1983: 12–13), *achira* (Ugent et al. 1984: 420–422), and manioc (Ugent et al. 1986: 87–89), are also moderately abundant to abundant in all cuts.

The relative frequencies of other plants are more variable. Avocado seeds are abundant in Cut 5, rare in Cut 3, and moderately abundant in Cuts 1 and 2 as well as 6, where they occur in the middle levels of the deposit. Peppers, mainly stems, are especially abundant in Cut 4 but relatively rare in Cuts 1 and 6; and guava occurs in moderate amounts in Cuts 1–4. Common beans occur sporadically in moderate (Cuts 4 and 6) or relatively rare quantities (Cuts 2 and 3), often in the same context as lima beans, which are moderately abundant in Cut 4 and relatively rare in Cuts 2, 3, and 6. Both types of beans occur predominantly in the middle natural levels of Cut 6. Three additional species, *pacae* (*Inga feuillei*), *cansaboca*, and *Canavalia* beans, occur very intermittently and in much smaller quantities. Despite their extreme rarity, they are important because they represent additional cultivated or tended species.

TORTUGAS

The early ceramic site of Tortugas is situated about 10 meters above sea level on the north side of Tortugas Bay, 11 kilometers north of the Casma Valley and slightly south of Huaynuná (fig. 2). Fung assigned the name Tortugas to this site in 1972, when she discussed the surface ceramics and their relationship with sites in the Casma area. However, this is not the preceramic site of Tortugas described by Thompson (1964a: 206) and Collier (1962: 411) and tested by Engel (1957a: 56, 1957b: 74–75). The preceramic site they describe is located just north of where the paved road from the Pan American Highway now reaches the edge of the bay (Donald Collier and Donald Thompson, personal communication). It has been badly damaged by local house construction since their reconnaissance.

Tortugas Bay is currently rimmed by the beach resort town of Tortugas, and local house and road construction has destroyed much of the early ceramic archaeological site of Tortugas. However, on the basis of conversations with local homeowners, we learned that many nearby houses were built on midden; and on the basis of this, we estimate the original areal extent of the site to have been about 1/2 hectare. The deepest zone of preserved midden lies southeast of a rocky ridge which projects into the bay. Testing in the main part of Tortugas was limited to three pits because of the small areal extent of undisturbed deposit, and we chose two of these pits for controlled stratigraphic excavation (Cuts 1 and 2).

We obtained three radiocarbon dates from charcoal collected in the two stratigraphic cuts. The two dates from Cut 1 are 2115 ± 65 B.C. (UGA-4523) and 2590 ± 200 B.C. (UGA-4524), and the one from Cut 2 is 1800 ± 65 B.C. (UGA-4525) (table 2). Two of these dates lie in the range of the Cotton Preceramic Period, whereas the third is at the transition between the Cotton Preceramic Period and the Initial Period. Since the artifact and subsistence inventories are closely paralleled at Pampa de las Llamas-Moxeke and point to a contemporaneous Initial Period date for Tortugas, the dates appear to be too early. It is possible that the charcoal dated was from old driftwood that inhabitants of Tortugas had used as fuel.

Architecture

Low stone walls are visible at several points where midden deposits were truncated during house and driveway construction. These walls are

Fig. 24. Portion of a circular domestic structure with a stone wall base and a silty clay floor found in a stratigraphic excavation (Cut 1) at the Initial Period site of Tortugas.

double-faced and made of cobbles with rubble fill. All are low, generally only three to four cobbles high. In stratigraphic Cut 1 (fig. 24) we encountered an arc of cobbles and boulders which formed part of a similar structure. Two superposed floors of fine, yellow, silty sand were associated with this small circular structure, and their distribution within the midden indicates that the structure was at least 130 centimeters in diameter and may have been constructed on top of a small mound. This and the other low-walled architecture were probably small domestic structures whose inhabitants were responsible for the local dense midden accumulation.

Testing along a small rocky spur within the site revealed part of a construction that probably did not have a domestic function. At this point, a small platform had been built, taking advantage of the rocky outcrop to enhance the structure's height. What remains of the platform consists of loose fill of very angular pebbles and cobbles quarried from the hillside. These are confined by loosely formed bags made of twisted and knotted reeds which were probably also used to transport the stone to

Fig. 25.   A second stratigraphic excavation (Cut 2) at Tortugas revealed a pebble floor plastered with silty clay overlying a platform of bagged fill. Excavation in the right half of the cut revealed the distribution of the rounded pebbles beneath the plaster.

the site. Such bagged fill is common inside nondomestic, often monumental, structures such as the main temple at Las Haldas, the restored building at El Paraíso, and the platform mounds of Aspero (Engel 1967: 50; Feldman 1980: 49; Matsuzawa 1978: 658; Moseley and Willey 1973: 460–461; Quilter 1985: 294–295). At Tortugas, this fill is capped by two successive well-formed floors of fine sand and silt 2 to 3 centimeters thick, separated by 5 to 10 centimeters of loose rocks and sand. The upper floor was prepared by laying a pavement of well-rounded pebbles 2 to 4 centimeters in diameter in coarse sand and covering them with a layer of plaster (fig. 25). We excavated a meter-square area (Cut 2) of the refuse above this floor by natural levels, and during this excavation we discovered a hearth associated with the upper floor. The hearth was roughly circular, at least 40 centimeters in diameter, and contained substantial amounts of wood charcoal. We derived the 1800 ± 65 B.C. date from this charcoal.

Artifacts

The ceramics of Tortugas closely resemble those of Pampa de las Llamas-Moxeke. The range of shape and decoration is more limited at Tortugas, but this may be the result of its smaller sample size. Vessel forms present at Tortugas are confined to neckless ollas and a few bowls. The neckless olla rims are very similar to the more angled ones recovered by Fung (1972: fig. 3a–b, g) during her survey of the site in 1968. The dominant decorative pattern, also seen at Pampa de las Llamas-Moxeke, is a line of large, deep, angular punctations situated along the angled shoulder of the body of neckless ollas (fig. 26; compare with Fung 1972: pl. 2c–f). Some incision is also present. The interiors of most sherds are well smoothed, like those of Pampa de las Llamas-Moxeke.

We found one polished stone vessel rim on the surface of Tortugas between our two controlled stratigraphic excavations. It is virtually identical to examples found at Pampa de las Llamas-Moxeke.

We recovered twined cotton and *junco* and woven cotton textiles at Tortugas. Textile preservation at the site is poor, so the examples are quite small and badly deteriorated. Other artifacts include several stone

Fig. 26. Ceramics from Tortugas showing the same type of large punctations and incised decoration found on ceramics from Pampa de las Llamas-Moxeke.

beads, beads made from *Prunum curtum* shells by removing the apexes, and a piece of cut *Choromytilus chorus* shell. A single small cactus-spine fishhook (fig. 5c) probably exemplifies a type of tackle used in addition to nets to capture the very small fish which are so abundant in the refuse.

Subsistence

Both animal and plant remains are very common and well preserved within the Tortugas midden. Shellfish are especially abundant, and the species present reflect a preference for collecting at the rocky shoreline that is immediately below the site. This habitat yielded smaller mussels from the tide zone and larger species from deeper water. The small mussels *Semimytilus algosus* and *Brachidontes purpuratus* were especially abundant within the levels of both cuts, and other rock-perching species, including the large mussel *Choromytilus chorus* and the gastropods *Crepidula dilatata*, *Thais chocolata*, and *Tegula atra*, and barnacles are abundantly represented in Cut 2 and moderately abundant in Cut 1. *Thais delessertiana*,.another gastropod, and tunicates occur in moderate abundance in both cuts, while the large mussel *Aulocomya ater* occurs in moderate amounts in Cut 2 but is relatively rare in Cut 1. Remains of crabs and sea urchins are relatively rare in both cuts, and additional rock-perching species of chiton and *Prunum curtum* occur relatively rarely in Cut 1 and Cut 2, respectively.

Protothaca thaca, occurring in moderate amounts in Cut 2 and relatively rarely in Cut 1, is the most abundant of the sand-dwelling species. Among the other clams, *Mesodesma donacium* is relatively rare in both cuts, while *Donax peruvianus* and *Semele corrugata* occur in relatively rare quantities in Cut 2. The scallop *Argopecten purpuratum* is relatively rare in both cuts. All these shellfish are considered significant because their remains were distributed throughout the natural strata of each midden cut unless otherwise indicated. Exceptions in this case are *Choromytilus chorus*, chiton, and *Protothaca thaca* remains from Cut 1 which are restricted to the upper levels. Remains of small fish are very common in the refuse and often consist of heads and especially sections of flesh which may have been dried and preserved locally.

Plant remains are both abundant and varied at Tortugas. Cotton remains are especially abundant, but unlike at Pampa de las Llamas-Moxeke, where there are other plant parts, we recovered primarily seeds and fiber at Tortugas. Gourd rinds and seeds are also predictably abun-

Fig. 27. Remains of tubers recovered from stratigraphic excavations at Tortugas.

dant, and both these industrial species, along with *lúcuma* and peanut, occurred abundantly in both cuts. One species of squash (*C. maxima*) was moderately abundant in both cuts, and we recovered peppers and lima beans in moderate amounts in Cut 1. Tubers (fig. 27), including potatoes (Ugent et al. 1982: 185–188, 1983: 7–9), sweet potatoes (Ugent et al. 1981: 405–406, 1983: 13–14), *jícama* (*Pachyrrhizus* sp.) (Ugent et al. 1981: 403, 1983: 7), and manioc (Ugent et al. 1986: 90–92), occur relatively rarely in Cut 1. We have also identified common beans, avocado, and guava among the domesticated plant species at Tortugas, but all are very rare and more sporadically distributed within the midden than the significant species discussed above. The inhabitants of Tortugas collected large amounts of marine algae, probably concurrently with shellfish procurement.

SAN DIEGO

The site of San Diego, located in the lower Casma Valley some 5.5 kilometers from the Pacific Ocean (fig. 2) and about 10 meters above sea level, was first recorded in 1937 by Tello, who later briefly described it

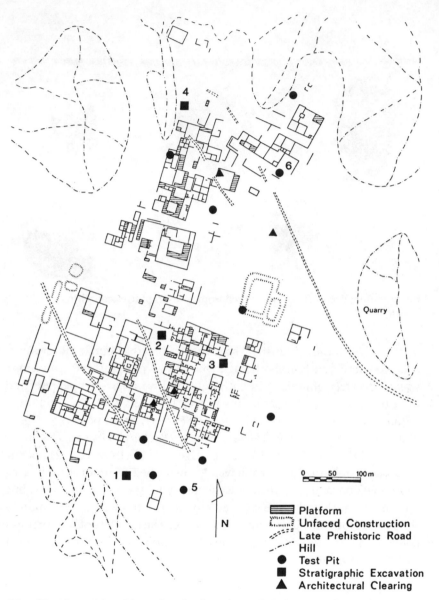

Fig. 28. Plan of San Diego showing locations of 1980 excavations. The site is comprised of small platform mounds associated with many rooms, courts, and plazas.

and dated it as "Sub-Chimu" (Tello 1956: 296–298). Thompson (1961: 74–75, 241–244, 1964a: 208) subsequently dated San Diego as a Middle Formative site, 750 to 400 B.C.

San Diego, the largest purely residential site preserved in the Casma Valley, extends over a flat area of about 50 hectares which is bordered by low granitic hills (fig. 28). In and around the architecture are substantial accumulations of midden up to 2 meters deep. Most of the site dates to the Early Horizon, with little sign of later intrusive material, but there are extensive looted cemeteries of later periods along the northern, southern, and western edges of the site. Several late prehistoric roads cross the site, both through and over buried early architecture.

We excavated a total of nineteen test pits at the site, four of which (fig. 28, Cuts 1–4) were expanded into 1-by-1-meter stratigraphic excavations and four of which were extended to investigate architecture. We obtained five radiocarbon dates from charcoal extracted from two of the stratigraphic cuts (table 2). The three dates from Cut 1 are 355 ± 55 B.C. (UGA-4513), 540 ± 60 B.C. (UGA-4512), and 560 ± 115 B.C. (UGA-4514). The two dates from Cut 4 are 295 ± 60 B.C. (UGA-4516) and 505 ± 70 B.C. (UGA-4517). All of these dates are within the Early Horizon and correlate with Thompson's dating of the site. The excavations recovered abundant subsistence and artifactual remains as well as encountering one burial that is associated with the main occupation of the site.

Architecture

Most of the site is covered by a series of interconnected architectural units including large and small rooms, corridors, plazas, courts, and small platform mounds (fig. 29). Unlike earlier sites in the Casma Valley, no single structure or mound dominates the site. All construction consists of angular cobbles and boulders quarried from nearby hillsides that have been wet-laid in silty clay mortar. Contrary to the descriptions of Tello (1956: 296), we encountered no rectangular adobes. The architecture for the most part shares a common magnetic orientation. North-south walls of the structure are oriented between 12 and 18 degrees east of north, whereas east-west walls are at right angles to that orientation. Most of the architecture is partially buried by windblown sand, and the northern half of the site appears more deeply buried than the southern half.

The most distinctive architectural feature is a low, narrow platform mound associated with a small court that is often entered by way of a baffled entrance. During survey we surmised that access to the summit

Fig. 29. General view of the architecture at San Diego from the southwest.

of each platform mound was gained by means of a pair of staircases, each located at opposite ends of the platform. However, excavation revealed that the access points are actually ramps bordered by low stone walls. Excavated ramps show signs of two or more construction phases. The summit of at least one platform contains a row of rectangular pillars measuring approximately 45 centimeters by 55 centimeters (fig. 30), and the summit of another platform contains the remains of a large wooden post, presumably also used as a roof support. Other areas of San Diego also have surface indications of wooden posts.

Test pits in the north half of the site revealed that almost completely buried court walls stand over 2 meters high. Associated with one court wall are low benches that were modified during various construction phases. Excavated architecture from all parts of the site shows signs of sloppy workmanship; crude plaster, often bearing numerous fingermarks, only partially covers most wall faces.

Finally, several test pits revealed fragmentary evidence of perishable domestic dwellings of wood and cane. One stratigraphic excavation off a test pit (Cut 4) revealed the corner of a *quincha* (wattle and daub) house supported on one side by a low stone wall (fig. 31).

Fig. 30. Small rectangular pillars found on the summit of one platform mound at San Diego.

Fig. 31. Remains of a buried *quincha* or cane house with a stone support wall found at the bottom of a stratigraphic excavation (Cut 4) at San Diego.

Burial

During excavation at San Diego we found one burial associated with the main occupation (figs. 28, 32), and we encountered it in a test pit (Cut 5) south of the main site architecture. Figure 32 shows a plan of this burial of an infant within a large ceramic olla which has a maximum diameter of 50 centimeters. We encountered the broken top-section of the vessel 40 centimeters below the modern ground surface. Although we found some olla body sherds in the sandy matrix within the vessel, no rim sherds were present. This indicates that the rim portion of the olla had been broken off before it was used as a burial container for the child. Even without the rim, other characteristics of the olla are coincident with ceramic collections from the remainder of the site.

The child's body had been placed in a seated position with its head bent forward in the direction magnetic N40°W. The infant's legs were bent in front of the body, with the knees pointing outward and the lower legs close but not crossed. Prior to excavation, some lateral movement of the upper torso had occurred such that the arms were slightly shifted from the original positions. The left arm was bent at about a 90-degree

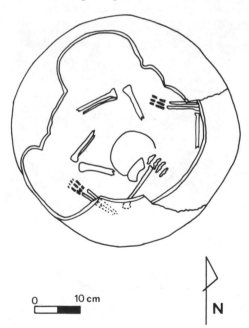

0   10 cm

N

Fig. 32. Plan of the flexed burial of an infant within a large broken olla found in Cut 5 at San Diego.

Fig. 33. Fragment of a combination neckless olla and short-neck jar rim found within the large olla containing the infant burial in Cut 5 at San Diego.

angle, with the left hand resting palm-up near the left leg. The right arm, situated farther from the vertebral column, was also bent at a 90-degree angle, with the right hand resting palm-up near the right leg. Analysis of the long bones and teeth of the infant indicates that its age at death was between six and twelve months.

No intact grave goods accompanied the infant, but within the sandy matrix of the vessel were several sherds and organic remains similar to the midden material encountered outside the vessel and in other excavations at the site. Among the ceramics collected from the olla matrix was a large sherd which combines the neck of a jar with the rim of a neckless olla (fig. 33). This puzzling find should serve as a cautionary reminder to analysts of early Peruvian ceramics, who normally visualize jar necks and neckless ollas as two totally separate forms. Similar vessel forms which are roughly contemporaneous with San Diego have been found at the highland sites of Kotosh (Izumi and Terada 1972: 183, 310–311, pl. 104: 18) and Huacaloma (Terada and Onuki 1982: 107, 255–256, pl. 93: 2–4, 6, 8, 9, 13).

Artifacts

Most numerous of the artifacts found were pottery sherds, both from midden deposits and associated with architecture. Vessel forms identi-

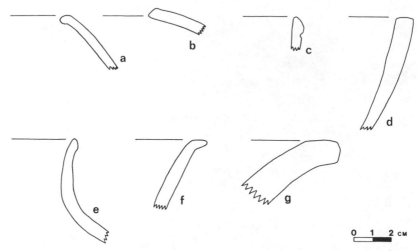

Fig. 34. Rim profiles of ceramic vessels from San Diego, including neckless ollas (*a*, *b*), a thick stirrup spout (*c*), a bowl (*d*), and jars (*e–g*).

Fig. 35. Fragments of ceramic panpipes found at San Diego.

fied at San Diego include neckless ollas, short-neck, tall-neck, and flaring-rim jars, bowls, grater bowls, and jars with thick stirrup spouts (fig. 34). Fragments of other forms reveal the existence of panpipes (fig. 35), solid figurines, spindle whorls, a club head (fig. 36), and reworked sherds made into perforated and unperforated pottery disks. The range of ceramic decoration encompasses incision, zoned and unzoned punctations, circle-and-dot designs (fig. 37), textile and net impressions on vessel exteriors (fig. 38), zoned white painted designs bordered by incised lines (fig. 39), appliqué knobs, and modeling. The interiors of virtually all sherds from constricted vessels were roughly smoothed when

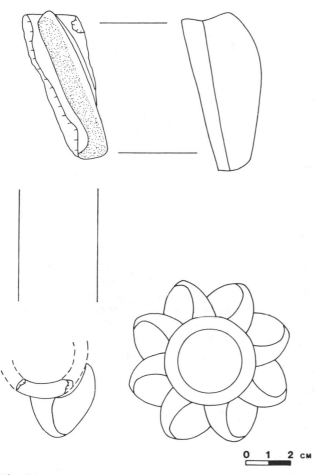

0   1   2 CM

Fig. 36. Multiple views and a reconstruction drawing of the fragmentary ceramic club head from San Diego.

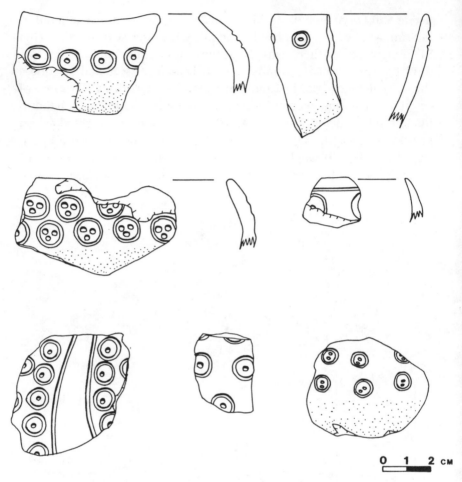

Fig. 37. Ceramics from the site of San Diego showing a variety of circle-and-dot designs as well as the vessel forms upon which they occur.

the clay was fairly dry, a process which left numerous irregular holes and cracks. The range of ceramic material found at San Diego shares characteristics with the Patazca style and associated pottery types described by Collier (1962: 412).

We found numerous other types of artifacts during excavation. Among these items are worked shell, beads, cane-impressed clay, a gourd container which may have been for lime, a spindle with thread, a sherd tied with string, and a broken *Thais chocolata* shell with string. Other artifacts that have more potential for cross-dating purposes are ground slate blades (fig. 40), two thorn fishhooks (fig. 5d–e), woven cotton

Fig. 38. Net and fabric impressions found on the exteriors of sherds at San Diego.

Fig. 39. Ceramics decorated with white paint outlined by incised lines found at San Diego.

Fig. 40. Fragments of polished slate blades found at San Diego.

textiles with blue and white geometric designs, bast knotless netting, and a cotton knitted bag.

Subsistence

Virtually all of the animal protein consumed at San Diego came from the ocean. The only nonmarine animal bones came from a fox or dog and from a rodent which was probably attracted to the refuse and later died. *Scutalus* sp., the local land snail, was consistently present, though relatively rare, in Cuts 1, 2, and 4, and was probably eaten. Marine species, mainly shellfish and some fish, attest to exploitation of the rocky areas as well as sandy beaches near modern Puerto Casma at the mouth of the river.

Most of the more abundant species are rock-perching types. These include the small mussels *Semimytilus algosus* and *Brachidontes purpuratus* as well as chitons, which are consistently present and abundantly represented within all four cuts. The small tide-zone clam *Donax peruvianus* is abundant in the natural strata of Cuts 2 and 4, moderate in frequency in Cut 1, and relatively rare in Cut 3. Littoral-zone species of crab and sea urchins, as well as barnacles, limpets, and the gastropod *Tegula atra*, occur in moderate frequencies in all four cuts, whereas the medium-sized clam *Mesodesma donacium* is moderately common in Cuts 1, 2, and 4, but relatively rare in Cut 3. Cut 4 also yielded moderate amounts of two additional gastropods, *Thais chocolata* and *Thais delessertiana*, as well as the razor clam, *Tagelus dombeii*, and the large mussel *Aulocomya ater*. *Tagelus dombeii* also occurs in moderate amounts in Cut 2 and relatively rarely in Cuts 1 and 3. *Thais delessertiana* also occurs relatively rarely in Cuts 1 and 2, whereas *Thais chocolata* is relatively rare in Cuts 2 and 3. The mussel *Aulocomya ater*, which inhabits deeper water, also occurs relatively rarely in Cut 1.

Other relatively rare species vary more in occurrence among the cuts. The scallop *Argopecten purpuratum* is relatively rare in Cuts 1 and 4, and the mud-flat clam, *Chione subrugosa*, is relatively rare in Cuts 1 and 2. *Turbo niger*, a gastropod, is relatively rare in Cut 2, where it occurs mainly in the upper levels. Along with the sand-dwelling clam *Protothaca thaca*, the rock-perching species *Choromytilus chorus*, *Crepidula dilatata*, and *Concholepas concholepas* are all relatively rare but consistently represented in Cut 4. *Chione subrugosa*, *Trachycardium procerum*, and *Tagelus dombeii*, three of the mud-dwelling species common to the nearby early preceramic site of Almejas (S. Pozorski and T. Pozorski 1981), occur in greatly reduced amounts at San Diego, but their presence suggests that at least a small colony of exotic warm-water species still existed locally.

Preservation is excellent at San Diego, and plant remains are extremely abundant. Our most substantial evidence of maize comes from San Diego and the very similar and contemporary site of Pampa Rosario. Maize (fig. 41) is one of the most frequently represented plants at San Diego. It is abundant in all four stratigraphic excavations, and one test pit (Cut 6) encountered a cache of fifty-one whole maize cobs with kernels adjacent to a stack of whole maize stalks. Both cobs and kernels are quite small, and the kernels are dark in color.

Gourd, cotton, and peanut remains are also relatively abundant in all cuts, indicating the importance of these plants at the site. All parts of the cotton plant as well as gourd seeds and rind fragments occur with great frequency. Common bean and lima bean remains (fig. 42) were abundant in Cut 1, and lima bean remains were moderately abundant in Cuts 2 and 4. Of the significant crop species, pepper was moderately frequent in Cuts 1 and 2; and tubers, including manioc (Ugent et al. 1986: 93–94) and *achira* (Ugent et al. 1984: 423–426), were moderately common in Cuts 1, 2, and 4. Squash (*C. maxima*) was consistently present but relatively rare in Cuts 1 and 4, and common bean remains were relatively rare in Cut 4. Guava and *pacae* were relatively rare in Cut 4. Four additional species, *Canavalia* beans (fig. 42), *lúcuma*, avocado, and *cansaboca*, were present but rare, and were not consistently represented within the natural strata. All are significant, however, as an indication

Fig. 41. Remains of maize cobs and plant parts found in midden excavations at San Diego.

Fig. 42. Remains of various types of beans found in midden excavations at San Diego.

of the range of species the inhabitants of San Diego exploited. The decreased quantities of *lúcuma* and avocado also suggest changing dietary preferences.

PAMPA ROSARIO

Pampa Rosario is a large settlement located at an elevation of 150 meters. It lies on a flat plain bordered by granitic hills near the confluence of the Sechin and Casma branches of the Casma Valley, some 16 kilometers inland from the Pacific Ocean (fig. 2). Collier and Thompson tested this site in 1956 by excavating two pits near the largest structure (Carlevato 1979: 39–42). They consider Pampa Rosario a Middle Formative site, dating roughly from 750 to 400 B.C. (Collier 1962: 414; Thompson 1961, 1964a: 207–208).

Pampa Rosario covers about 40 hectares and consists of over twenty principal structures interspersed with areas of midden 0.5 to over 2 meters deep (fig. 43). Most of the site dates to the Early Horizon, but some later constructions and canals have disturbed parts of the Early Horizon occupation. Time constraints limited our investigations to surface survey of the entire site and the excavation of ten test pits into middens, one of which (fig. 43, Cut 1) we expanded into a 1-by-1-meter stratigraphic excavation to recover subsistence and chronological information. Three radiocarbon dates run on charcoal obtained from Cut 1 are 450 ± 70 B.C. (UGA-4536), 585 ± 75 B.C. (UGA-4537), and 810 ± 75 B.C. (UGA-4535) (table 2). These dates agree with Collier and Thompson's dating of the site. The two later dates are contemporary with dates from San Diego, whereas the oldest date is within the range of dates from the postprimary Early Horizon midden at Las Haldas.

Architecture

All of the Early Horizon structures within Pampa Rosario are made of granitic rock set in silty clay mortar. The rock was quarried mainly from a small hill located in the southwestern corner of the site, and the silty clay for the mortar was probably obtained from nearby canals in either the Sechin or Casma branches of the Casma Valley or within the river beds themselves. The architecture is very reminiscent of structures present at the coastal site of San Diego, which dates to the same time period. Pampa Rosario architecture consists of low, narrow platform mounds associated with small courtyards and other connected rooms (figs. 43, 44).

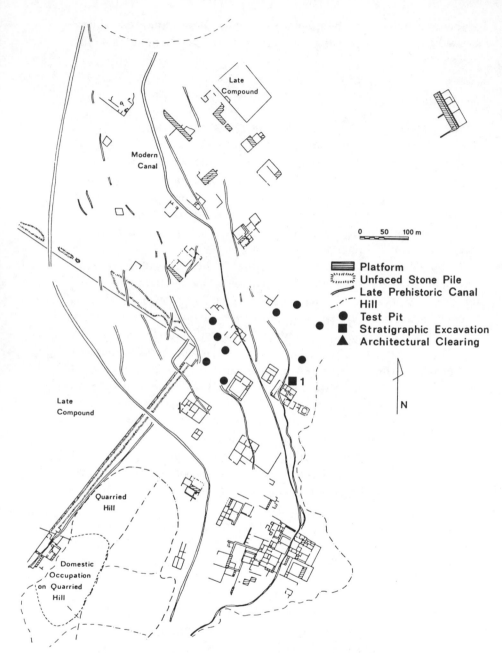

Fig. 43. Plan of the Early Horizon site of Pampa Rosario showing locations of 1980 excavations. The site consists of small platform mounds associated with rooms, courts, and plazas. It has been disturbed by later prehistoric compounds and canal excavations.

Fig. 44. General view of the largest preserved architectural complex at Pampa Rosario from the northeast.

As at San Diego, access to the summit of each low platform mound is gained by means of a pair of low ramps located at opposite ends of the platform mound. The associated courtyard of each platform mound is often entered by means of a baffled entryway. One of these platform-courtyard-room complexes, located at the southern end of the site, is larger than the rest, but this may be because of preservation, since the northern half of the site has been much more severely affected by sheet-wash from infrequent El Niño floods. Like that at San Diego, the Pampa Rosario architecture appears primarily domestic in nature, with internal differences perhaps reflecting certain degrees of social status.

One curious structure is an isolated, narrow platform mound in the northeast corner of the site, some 300 meters away from any other construction (fig. 43). The mound is larger than other platforms, measuring about 80 meters long and only 15 meters wide, and ranging from 1 to 3 meters high. Like similar smaller platform mounds within the main part of the site, this platform mound has two low inset ramps at opposite ends that lead to the summit. Unlike the other platform mounds, however, it possesses a narrow, central freestanding ramp, perpendicular to the mound face, that leads up to the summit. Off the southeast end of the platform mound is a low, ramplike wall which is constructed so that it may have provided access to the summit as well. Behind the mound is a series of four rooms formed by low stone walls. This platform mound is consistent with the architectural parameters of the site, but because of its exceptional size, unique ramp system, and isolated position, it may have had a special ceremonial meaning for the inhabitants of Pampa Rosario.

Some later construction is also present at the site. On the north end is a large compound (fig. 43) made of rectangular adobes which probably dates from after the Early Intermediate Period. More prominent is a huge compound which occupies much of the western portion of the site (fig. 43). The northeast and southwest walls share alignments with other portions of the site. However, these long walls are not finished but are instead large, unfaced stone piles that contain numerous early sherds. They apparently represent the clearing away by later people of earlier structures once within the compound walls. This large compound is also aligned with, and was probably once connected to, three mound-and-courtyard complexes (not shown in fig. 43) within modern cultivation that date to the Early Intermediate Period or later.

Finally, coursing through much of the site are numerous segments of late prehistoric canals, probably dating to the Late Intermediate Period, that cut the large western compound as well as the Early Horizon structures. In 1980 a large concrete-lined canal was cut through the site to carry water from the Casma branch to the Sechin branch of the valley. This canal follows a prehistoric canal for much of its length, though the canal it follows was originally meant to carry water in the opposite direction. During the building of this modern canal, much of the site along the canal path was leveled for use as bank fill. Along the western canal bank, creation of a road has destroyed a strip from 10 to 50 meters wide.

Artifacts

The artifacts of Pampa Rosario, like the architecture, are very similar to those of San Diego. As in other ceramic sites of the Casma Valley, pottery sherds are the most common artifacts. The vessel forms at the site include neckless ollas, short-neck, tall-neck, and flaring-rim jars, bowls, grater bowls, bottles, and jars with thick stirrup spouts (fig. 45) which are like examples from San Diego. Panpipes, solid figurines, spindle whorls, and reworked pottery disks are common as well. Ceramic decoration duplicates techniques documented at San Diego—incision, zoned

Fig. 45. Fragments of thick, undecorated stirrup spouts found at Pampa Rosario.

and unzoned punctations, circle-and-dot designs, textile and net impressions on vessel exteriors, zoned white painted designs bordered by incised lines, appliqué knobs, and modeling. The same rough finishing of constricted vessel interiors that was notable at San Diego is also present at Pampa Rosario.

Other artifacts found at Pampa Rosario also link the site to San Diego. These include ground slate blades and woven cotton textiles with blue and white geometric designs. Additional artifacts from Pampa Rosario are a thorn needle, a repaired gourd fragment, and a polished stone vessel rim fragment which is very similar to examples found at Pampa de las Llamas-Moxeke. This polished stone vessel fragment, found on the site surface, could belong to the occupation of Pampa Rosario or could have been derived from the earlier occupation at Pampa de las Llamas-Moxeke on the opposite side of Cerro San Francisco, where stone vessel fragments are much more common.

Subsistence

At the inland site of Pampa Rosario, both marine and terrestrial species contributed to the animal-food portion of the diet. Marine animals include mainly shellfish, but fish were also important. Shellfish remains include abundant quantities of *Semimytilus algosus* and *Brachidontes purpuratus*, moderate amounts of chiton, barnacles, and limpets, and relatively small amounts of crab, sea urchin, *Tegula atra*, and *Thais delessertiana*—all of which are rock-perching species. *Thais delessertiana* occurs mainly in the lower portion of the stratigraphic excavation. Other significant species include *Mesodesma donacium*, a clam which occurs in moderate amounts, *Donax peruvianus*, a tide-zone clam which is relatively rare, and relatively small quantities of the scallop *Argopecten purpuratum*. The additional presence of *Tagelus dombeii*, especially, as well as other very rare and sporadically represented species, ties this site with San Diego and suggests that the coastal zone near Puerto Casma may have been the source of Pampa Rosario's seafood. *T. dombeii* was quite common for the duration of Almejas (S. Pozorski and T. Pozorski 1981), and was apparently still available, though not so common, during the exploitation of the area by the inhabitants of San Diego. A single fragment of *Spondylus* sp. shell was certainly a luxury item obtained from much farther north.

Pampa Rosario middens contain remains of camelids, probably llamas (*Lama glama*)—both skeletal evidence and dung. Foxes or dogs and guinea pigs (*Cavia porcellus*) may also have been eaten. Preliminary evidence does not suggest that land mammals were as important as marine products, but they certainly represent a significant contribution to the local diet. Land snails, another inland protein source, were among the most abundant mollusks at Pampa Rosario.

Plant remains from Pampa Rosario are abundant, and a great range of cultigens is represented. Predominant agricultural plants which are both consistently present and abundant include maize, cotton, gourd, peanuts, lima and common beans, and the tree fruit *cansaboca*. Pepper, guava, and avocado occur in moderate amounts, and remains of avocado appear to be concentrated in the lower levels of the stratigraphic excavation. Significant species which occur relatively rarely are squash (*C. maxima*), *Canavalia* beans (especially in the lower levels), and tubers, including manioc (Ugent et al. 1986: 92–93) and *achira* (Ugent et al. 1984: 423). Remains of *lúcuma* and *pacae* are also very rare and sporadic here. Apparently *lúcuma* was consumed less frequently by inhabitants of Pampa Rosario than by earlier people within the Casma Valley. We noted a similar decline in *lúcuma* remains at the site of San Diego, and this serves as additional evidence of the close ties between the two sites.

3

Early Sites Surveyed within the Casma Valley

As part of this study of early Casma Valley prehistory, we carried out intensive survey at a number of early sites within the valley. Collier and Thompson explored and described the major sites of the lower valley as part of their work in 1956 (Collier 1962; Thompson 1961, 1962a, 1964a). A more recent reconnaissance of the Sechin branch of the valley by Fung and Williams (1977) resulted in the discovery and description of additional sites located farther upvalley than the scope of Collier and Thompson's exploration. Our surveys of the zone since 1978 have focused on major sites which previous investigators characterized as early on the basis of architectural and/or ceramic evidence. These include Sechin Alto, Sechin Bajo, and Taukachi-Konkan in the central lower valley; Chankillo, La Cantina, and Pallka in the Casma branch of the river; and Huerequeque and Huaca Desvio in the Sechin branch of the river. Though we did not intensively survey the well-known Casma Valley site of Cerro Sechin, we also describe it in this section. The surveyed sites are presented in a chronological arrangement, starting with what we believe are the earlier sites and ending with later ones.

SECHIN ALTO

Sechin Alto is located entirely within the limits of modern cultivation, yet its visible remains cover almost 2 square kilometers (fig. 46). It lies immediately south of the Sechin River in the Sechin branch of the Casma Valley, at an elevation of about 125 meters and at a distance of 15 kilometers from the Pacific Ocean (fig. 2). The enormous central mound structure, which measures about 300 meters by 250 meters by 44 meters high, is the largest such mound in the New World for its time period. Kosok (1965: 214–215) appreciated the great size of this construction during his 1949–50 visit to the area:

One day, late in the afternoon, Señor Luna insisted upon showing us "*una huaca muy grande.*" Although fatigued, we obeyed
the call of duty and followed him to a site known locally as Las
Huacas de Monte Grande, just off the main road in the Sechin
Valley and some five miles from the town of Casma. We ap-
proached what, at first, appeared to be a huge natural mound of
stones and dirt. But after climbing to the top, we found it to be a
fairly well-preserved artificial mound! It had a semi-amphitheatre
type of arrangement within the top, which was partly hollowed
out on one side. We had found pyramids of this type in other valleys, but were astonished to find so large a mound in such a small
valley. Directly south of it was a similar mound, but in a poorer
state of preservation.

As we were about to leave, Señor Luna pointed to an enormous
adjacent mass of stones and dirt and said, "But, Señor, this is the
main *huaca.*" At first we refused to believe him for it seemed in-
credible that so huge a hill could be man-made! Our curiosity
again aroused, we dragged ourselves up the mound in a rather
skeptical and tired frame of mind. But after climbing up and
down its many platforms constructed on different levels, we finally became convinced that Señor Luna uttered an understate-
ment when he said, "*una huaca muy grande.*"

Tello (1956: 79–82) as well as Thompson (1961: 201–206, 1962a: 294,
1964a: 207–208) describe the principal structure as well as the set of
nearby outlying mounds which includes the examples Kosok so vividly
recorded. Although many of the features of the main mound have been
obscured by looting, the form is clearly U-shaped. Its alignment is magnetic E32°N, and the main entrance is upvalley toward the northeast.
All of the outlying mounds are coincident with respect to orientation,
and most examples with distinguishable features are also generally U-
shaped. The construction material for the Sechin Alto mounds consists
mainly of granitic blocks quarried from hillsides about 2 kilometers to
the south, all of which have been wet-laid with silty clay mortar. Many
of these blocks, especially along the main mound face, are huge, measuring over 1.5 meters. Sechin Alto and its associated mounds lie well
within the modern limits of cultivation, and this agricultural activity is
constantly eroding many of the smaller mounds and plaza boundaries.
It certainly has long since destroyed or buried the domestic occupation
which probably existed in the area.

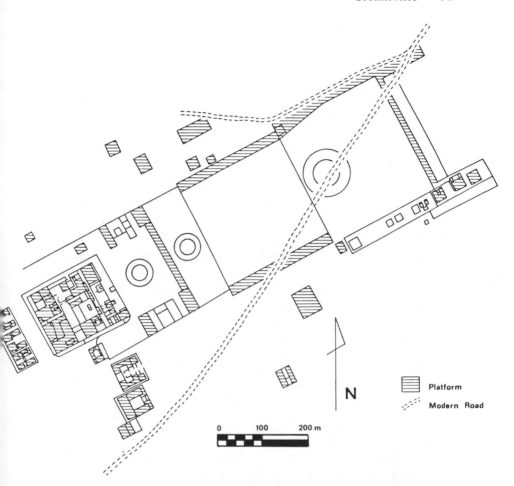

Fig. 46. Plan of Sechin Alto. The main mound is associated with four large plazas and three sunken circular forecourts.

Massive looting in the center of the main mound has obscured much of the mound top and left a gaping hole about 20 meters deep. A conical adobe core was thereby revealed, and component bricks can be observed in their original positions. The adobe portion of Sechin Alto may be a separate construction phase which predates the stone-faced construction currently so readily visible. Recent looting exposed a frieze remnant near the periphery of the adobe core, and this suggests that the adobe portion of Sechin Alto may once have been a free-standing mound adorned with mud sculpture.

Tello (1956: 79–82) and Thompson (1961: 201–206) describe a single large plaza immediately in front of the main mound. However, Fung and Williams (1977), with the aid of aerial photographs, were able to define a series of at least four plazas which extend northeast about 1400 meters in front of the main mound entrance. Sunken circular courts are clearly visible both on air photographs and on the ground in the second and fourth plazas from the main mound, and air-photograph evidence suggests that a third example is probably present in the first plaza. Thompson (1961: 204, 1964a: 207–208) recorded a stone monolith in the center of this court adjacent to the main mound. The new paved highway to Huaraz transects the largest of the three Sechin Alto circles (fig. 46). This feature of circular courts aligned with the main mound axis and within plazas is reminiscent of the architectural form of the visible Initial Period temple of Las Haldas.

Tello (1956: 82–83) recognized the early architectural form of Sechin Alto, which he compared to Chavin de Huantar, and went on to suggest that the late pottery on the site's surface did not accurately date the structures, but that massive excavation was necessary to reach the early ceramic levels. The only excavated ceramic samples from Sechin Alto come from six test pits made by Collier and Thompson in 1956 (Carlevato 1979: 29–39). In one of these pits on the summit of a mound south of the main huaca, they encountered 125 centimeters of refuse containing ceramics which they defined as Cahuacucho, overlain by 375 centimeters of refuse with Gualaño ceramics (Collier 1962: 411). The chronological relationship between the Cahuacucho and Gualaño ceramic styles has been questioned because both radiocarbon dates— 690 ± 90 B.C. for Cahuacucho and 1450 ± 100 B.C. for Gualaño (Berger et al. 1965: 347)—and thermoluminescent dates—approximately 800 B.C. for Cahuacucho and about 1000 B.C. for Gualaño (Mazess and Zimmerman 1966: 347–348)—contradict the stratigraphic evidence of Collier and Thompson (Bueno and Samaniego 1969: 34; Fung and Williams 1977: 132). During our examination of Collier and Thompson's ceramic collections at the Field Museum of Natural History, we noted a necklessolla sherd with deep gouges on the shoulder within the collection of Gualaño material (see also Carlevato 1979: 85). This sherd, as well as other plain sherds, is comparable to our ceramic samples from Pampa de las Llamas-Moxeke. Fung (1969: 186) has also reported similarities between the Gualaño material and ceramics from her phases 2 and 3 of the pretemple Initial Period occupation of Las Haldas. These factors support an interpretation of the Gualaño material as very early.

Ceramics of the style Collier and Thompson designated as Patazca were also found on the surface of the main mound, but not in subsurface excavations (Donald Collier, personal communication). This ceramic assemblage contains elements such as panpipes which are clearly associated with later single-component sites in the valley, such as Pampa Rosario and San Diego.

It would seem, then, that the status of chronological interpretations of Sechin Alto roughly parallels that of Las Haldas: the main mound seems to defy dating. The only excavations at Sechin Alto penetrated mound fill at points adjacent to later facades—well away from the main mound center where earlier constructions are most likely to be present. One of these excavations yielded very early ceramics associated with a radiocarbon date of about 1500 B.C., thereby suggesting the existence of an early local occupation during a time span that overlaps with those of both Pampa de las Llamas-Moxeke and pretemple Las Haldas. As was true for Las Haldas, there are no clear ceramic associations with the Sechin Alto mound and plaza constructions that are currently most visible. However, the end point of this massive construction phase is bracketed somewhat by the presence of later Early Horizon sherds on the mound surface in much the same way as the Las Haldas temple parameters are partially defined by the presence of the posttemple squatterlike occupation.

TAUKACHI-KONKAN

Slightly northwest of the site of Sechin Alto, and clearly visible from the surface of its main mound, is an expanse of plain bordered by Cerro Taukachi on the west and Cerro Konkan on the east. This plain is approximately 150 meters above sea level. Although the clusters of mounds and plazas on either edge of the plain were formerly treated as separate sites (Thompson 1961: 211–217), an examination of air photographs reveals a set of connected and associated architectural features which spans the pampa (Fung and Williams 1977: 116–118). The total complex of Taukachi-Konkan covers an area about 1250 meters by 500 meters (fig. 47). Most of the structures are constructed of granitic blocks quarried from nearby hillsides; all of the blocks have been set in silty clay mortar. Thompson (1961: 217) as well as Fung and Williams (1977: 116) have compared aspects of the form of this site with Sechin Alto. Taking this comparison a step further, we can see Taukachi-Konkan as furnishing

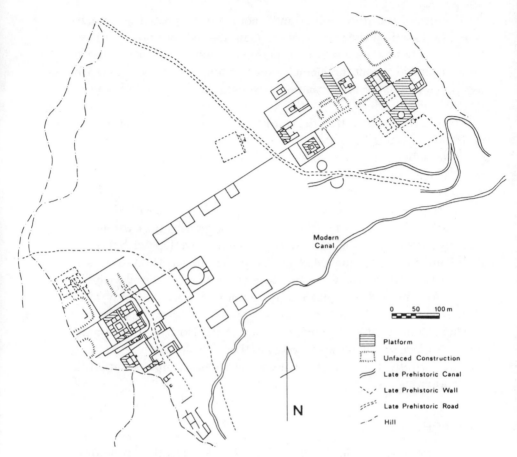

Fig. 47. Plan of Taukachi-Konkan, which consists of numerous large mounds and sunken circular courts.

evidence of features that might well have existed at Sechin Alto but are now obscured by centuries of cultivation encroaching on the larger site.

The principal mound of Taukachi-Konkan lies against Cerro Taukachi on the west, taking advantage of the sloping *cerro* base to enhance its height. It is most directly associated with another small U-shaped mound immediately to the south, a square mound in the rear which has an unfaced upper section, and an entirely unfaced artificial mound to the northwest. The top of the main mound has a U-shaped configuration, and it faces an associated series of plazas which extend northeast in line with the central mound axis at a magnetic orientation of E32°N.

These include an approximately square plaza immediately in front of the main mound, plus two circular courts: one created within a built-up platform adjacent to the square plaza and another, 480 meters away, which may also have been constructed within a built-up area. An even larger enclosure is formed by rows of low platforms and occasional connecting walls on either side of the central axis which are reminiscent of the winglike constructions of Sechin Alto.

The cluster of structures near Cerro Konkan is dominated by an unfaced, flat-topped, artificial mound about 90 meters on a side (fig. 47). More distinctive structures at this end of the site include a well-formed U-shaped mound which is aligned with other platforms, forming the greatly extended north wing of the main mound. This small mound faces a circular court immediately in front that is quite near the second circle of the principal mound. Two other medium-sized mounds form part of the east end of the site. The larger is associated with a square plaza and a raised platform containing a circle, thus forming a smaller version of the architectural components associated with the main mound at the site.

Taukachi-Konkan has been greatly affected by a later, probably Late Intermediate Period, occupation of the same pampa. The construction of late walls, roads, and compounds altered the configuration of several structures at the site (fig. 47). Large boulders from early constructions were torn out and used as grinding stones, and Late Intermediate Period ceramics are scattered over the entire pampa surface.

Taukachi-Konkan has been assigned an early date solely on the basis of architectural similarities to other early mounds and mound complexes because none of the investigators, ourselves included, encountered early ceramics at the site. On the basis of layout and form, Taukachi-Konkan has been compared to Chavin de Huantar and Pallka (Tello 1956: 75) as well as to the more similar complex of Sechin Alto (Fung and Williams 1977: 116; Thompson 1961: 217). Ceramic evidence of the early component of Taukachi-Konkan may have been obscured by the later extensive Late Intermediate Period reoccupation. However, this absence of early ceramics coupled with evidence of incomplete architectural features suggests that the early occupation of Pampa Taukachi-Konkan was brief. Thompson (1961: 212) and Fung and Williams (1977: 116, 118) noted the unfaced character of mounds and some walls at the site. Such unfaced portions of Taukachi-Konkan are clearly unfinished. The fact that important structures such as the top of the platform behind the main mound and the largest mound in the eastern sector were not completed suggests that Taukachi-Konkan ceased to be occupied before local construction could be fully realized as planned.

SECHIN BAJO

Sechin Bajo lies north of the Sechin River on the west side of Cerro Taukachi and about 1.2 kilometers southwest of Taukachi-Konkan (fig. 2). The site is about 120 meters above sea level, occupying a relatively flat pampa which is currently just outside of modern cultivation limits. It has been surveyed by Thompson (1961: 221–224) and Fung and Williams (1977: 118–120). (Tello [1956: 289–290, pl. 32] describes a site called Sechin Bajo, but this is a mound of rectangular adobes, dating to a later time period, which is located closer to the Sechin River than the site we describe as Sechin Bajo.)

The main structure of Sechin Bajo is a large mound of angular stones set in mud mortar, which measures about 150 meters by 110 meters by 16 meters high (fig. 48). Its form is a symmetrical U opening toward the northeast, with the central portion of the mound always lower than the sides, even at the back. On the north side of the first (easternmost) central court is a series of large, rectangular stone slabs which were probably intended for use as lintels. Several of the rectangular platforms atop the mound are unfaced, consisting of well-shaped but otherwise unrestrained piles of granules and pebbles. The structure is oriented magnetic E32°N, and along the central axis are two circular courts, one 70 meters and the other 230 meters from the main mound. From a study of the air photograph, a pair of slightly splayed-out wings can be discerned emanating from the main mound and bounding the nearer circle.

The pampa which contains Sechin Bajo was also reoccupied, probably during the Late Intermediate Period. A sizable late compound (Thompson 1961: 218–221) occupies the portion of this pampa northeast of Sechin Bajo, and walls associated with this compound run over the southern part of the early mound and obscure some of the construction details. Correspondingly late ceramics occur over all the pampa surface.

Sechin Bajo, like Taukachi-Konkan, is assigned an early date on the basis of architectural similarities to other early sites. No early ceramics have been found associated with Sechin Bajo, but Thompson (1961: 224) compared its form to Huaca A of Pampa de las Llamas-Moxeke, and it is especially similar in layout to Sechin Alto and Taukachi-Konkan. As was argued for Taukachi-Konkan, the unfaced and therefore unfinished

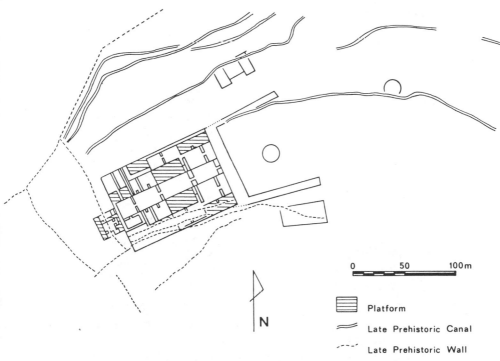

Fig. 48. Plan of Sechin Bajo, which has small wing structures and two sunken courts.

state of major parts of the Sechin Bajo mound surface suggests that construction at this site was also never completed. Consequently, the occupation was brief and the paucity of ceramics is a predictable result.

CERRO SECHIN

Cerro Sechin, the most famous of the sites within the Casma Valley, is located at the base of a large granite hill near the juncture of the Sechin and Casma branches of the valley, some 13 kilometers from the Pacific Ocean (fig. 2). This area has an elevation of about 100 meters. The main structure of the site measures 50 meters square and is small by comparison to other early ceramic sites in the Casma area. This central structure, which has rounded corners, is famous for the carved monoliths that line its facade on all four sides. Various investigators have periodically excavated the structure since 1937 (Bueno and Samaniego 1969; Collier 1962; Samaniego 1973; Tello 1943, 1956), and it has received more attention than any other mound in the valley. The age of Cerro Sechin has been a topic of controversy for years, but recent investigations (Samaniego et al. 1985) have helped to more firmly establish the chronological position of at least part of the site.

Two problems are central to the dating of Cerro Sechin. First, some confusion surrounds the ordering of various construction phases at the site. Very generally, there are two basic temple structures, an inner one with at least two phases of conical adobe construction and an outer one which is adorned by the famous carved monoliths. Both early excavators, Tello (1943: 144–145, 1956: 280) and Collier (1962: 414), believe that the central conical adobe temple structure postdates the outer carved monolith structure. Samaniego (1973: 45–51), the most recent investigator, has defined three construction phases of the adobe structure, all of which he feels are earlier than the carved monolith structure which constitutes a fourth construction phase. Superposed central staircases belonging to the various construction phases are plainly visible today, and they provide convincing evidence that Samaniego's sequence is generally correct.

The second, more serious, problem concerns the associations of ceramics and other artifacts with the various construction phases. None of the construction phases, including the carved monolithic outer face, has firm artifactual or ceramic associations. Tello (1943: 144, 1956: 280) felt that the monoliths had been reused by people using "Sub-Chavin" pottery, which he defines as the second period of Chavin pottery and which some authors interpret as post-Chavin (Willey 1971: 112). Kroeber (1944: 50–52, pl. 22) remains noncommittal about Cerro Sechin, and the ceramics he illustrated from surface collections are all Casma Incised pottery, which is now known to date to a later time period (C. Daggett 1983: 22). Collier (1962: 414) found no sherds in his excavations within the central adobe temple. Thompson (1964a: 208) dates the site as Middle Formative, 750 to 450 B.C., on the basis of Patazca ceramics found there (though he does not specify by whom) and by the presence of conical adobe construction. Bueno and Samaniego (1969: 34) found nine sherds in the fill of the floor associated with the base of the carved monoliths, thus showing that the carvings at least belong to a pottery period. On the basis of the similarities between their ceramics and Collier's (1962: 412) Cahuacucho pottery, as well as sherds from Las Haldas, Bueno and Samaniego (1969: 31–34) suggest the site may date as early as 1600 B.C. Later, Samaniego (1973: 71–72) indicates that in a stratum of refuse overlying the floor associated with the monoliths there are fragments of poorly fired Las Haldas type figurines that are associated with the earliest Chavin occupations at the site. On this basis, he suggests that the monoliths are pre-Chavin, dating to about 1500 B.C.

Recently, Samaniego et al. (1985: 182–184) have published the best evidence to date for the age of the carved monoliths. They obtained one radiocarbon date of 1290 ± 20 B.C. and a thermoluminescent date of 1290 ± 240 from a burned post associated with the use of the monoliths. This late Initial Period dating of the monoliths supports the arguments of Collier (1962: 414), Lanning (1967: 93), and Willey (1971: 112), who felt that the style of the stone carvings was pre-Chavin, dating before the beginning of the Rowe (1962, 1967) Chavin art style seriation. Conversely, it does not support the very late Chavin stylistic dating Lathrap (1971: 74) and Roe (1974: 34–36) proposed for the monoliths.

In addition to the recently published radiocarbon date, architectural traits and unpublished ceramic evidence help define the time span of occupation of the site. In terms of architecture, the presence of an inner conical adobe construction is reminiscent of the conical adobe construction in the interior of Sechin Alto. As noted previously, ceramic associations at Cerro Sechin have been rarely published, but unpublished evidence provided by Segundo Vasquez (personal communication) offers some clues as to at least the duration of occupation at the site. Vasquez conducted his own excavation in the passageway along the west side of the main structure in 1976 and analyzed the excavated material for his B.A. thesis at the University of Trujillo. He also analyzed ceramics from the excavations Samaniego had directed in the early 1970s. Though the material analyzed to date all comes from fill and deposition between 20 centimeters and over 4 meters above the floor associated with the monoliths, the evidence is still useful. A single sherd recovered has large punctations like those of Pampa de las Llamas-Moxeke and Tortugas. Other more common ceramic decoration—including incision, punctation, and zoned punctation—is reminiscent of ceramics from Las Haldas. Also present are later ceramic traits such as circle-and-dot designs, panpipes, and possibly combination neckless-olla / short-neck-jar rims which are found at San Diego and Pampa Rosario. Though still inconclusive, this ceramic evidence, in combination with the architectural evidence, indicates that the occupation at Cerro Sechin lasted from the early Initial Period well into the Early Horizon.

The subject matter of the carved monoliths may be useful in dating the site. It has been proposed that the warrior figures, severed heads, and dismembered body parts represent (1) a laboratory center for anatomical studies (Paredes 1975), (2) a center for a fertility rite (Wickler and

Seibt (1982: 442–443), (3) a center for human sacrifices (Kauffmann 1980: 194–195), or (4) the commemoration of a decisive battle of one group with another (Alarco 1975: 5; Jimenez Borja 1969: 39)—either an external group conquering a local population (Bueno and Samaniego 1969: 33) or a local Sechin group conquering another group in the Casma Valley (Samaniego 1973: 70–71). Of all the possibilities, the battle commemoration hypothesis seems most plausible, and evidence from our investigations at other Casma Valley sites tends to support the external conquest hypothesis.

SECHIN ALTO COMPLEX

The similarity in mound forms and site layout of Sechin Alto, Taukachi-Konkan, and Sechin Bajo has been used to argue that Taukachi-Konkan and Sechin Bajo are early sites despite their lack of associated early ceramics. Carrying this argument further, we propose that such similarity of form and layout combined with the coincidental orientation of all three sites both provides evidence of contemporaneity of the sites and suggests that they may once have formed part of a single, large, continuous settlement which occupied land on both sides of the Sechin River but is now interrupted by modern cultivation. The Initial Period occupation of Cerro Sechin is also believed to be part of this large settlement because of the use of conical adobes in its inner-temple structures, making it similar to Sechin Alto, and because of the site's proximity to Sechin Alto, Sechin Bajo, and Taukachi-Konkan. We have designated these four juxtaposed sites the Sechin Alto Complex. The distance between the component mounds suggests that the Sechin Alto Complex was at least 10.5 square kilometers in area. The architectural tenets of U-shaped mounds and inner conical adobe structures in combination with a well-aligned series of multiple circular courts and square or rectangular plazas are seen to express a single, relatively brief, but cohesive development represented physically by Taukachi-Konkan, Sechin Bajo, Cerro Sechin, and the final and most visible major construction phase at Sechin Alto.

HUEREQUEQUE

The site of Huerequeque is located about 24 kilometers inland at an elevation of 425 meters on the north bank of the Sechin River. It has been described by Williams (1972) in a discussion of circular forecourts and by Fung and Williams (1977: 123) as part of their survey of the Sechin branch of the river. Huerequeque (fig. 49) consists of a large central mound and plaza complex plus small, irregular, domestic structures associated with thin patches of midden—all of which cover approximately 35 hectares of the sloping hillside. Component structures were fabricated from cobbles and boulders readily available on the nearby slopes. The adjacent hillside is quite bare of larger stones and shows evidence of this quarrying.

The main mound is generally square in form and faces magnetic E18°S, overlooking the Sechin Valley. The top of the mound is symmetrically subdivided into a series of rooms, and four very large rectangular blocks of stone, which probably served as lintels, still lie near the central entrance up onto the main mound. Mound construction clearly took advantage of the steeply sloping hillside to enhance the apparent height of this central structure. Behind and separate from the main mound is a series of three small contiguous rooms with rounded corners. A square plaza and an adjoining circular one extending toward the valley floor complete the complex. In response to the gradient of the hillslope, the downslope peripheries of both plazas are substantially built up. This is especially true of the circular court which has walls that are greatly thickened to achieve the desired height of about 3 meters (fig. 50). At first glance, it may seem peculiar that this circular court is a construction built on top of a hillslope rather than a hole excavated into the ground. However, close examination of other circular courts within and outside the Casma Valley reveals that most are either excavated into artificially raised surfaces or excavated only slightly into natural ground but look deeply excavated because their perimeters have been built up with artificial fill.

Parts of Huerequeque have been substantially altered by later prehistoric agricultural development of the zone. Numerous small canals transect the area, and one even cuts through the central structure between the main mound and the square plaza (fig. 49). Associated construction undoubtedly transformed much of the early domestic architecture into agricultural terraces. These intrusive terraces are quite clear, however, because of their long, narrow form, their association with canals, and the presence of late sherds of the type defined by Collier (1962: 416) as Casma Incised.

Early ceramics occur mainly above the highest canal in areas unaffected by later terracing, as well as near the main structure. The neckless olla was the only vessel form we observed, and the only decorated

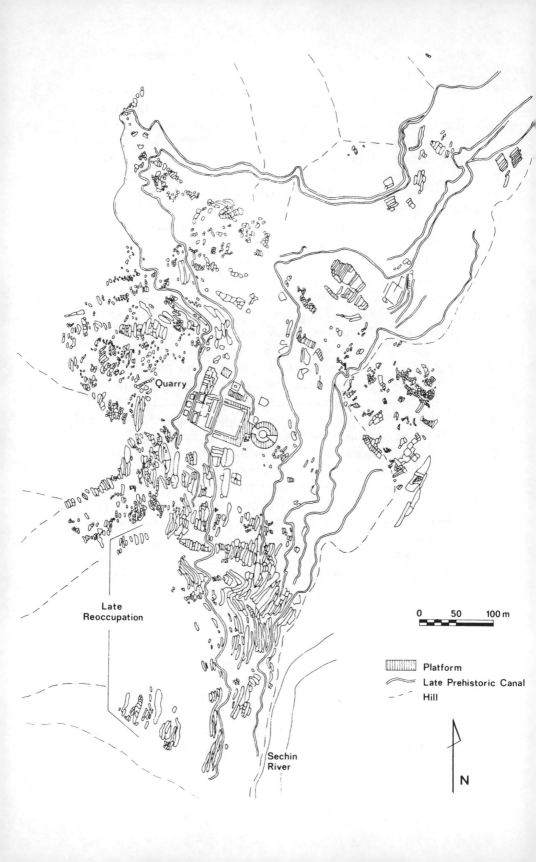

Quarry

Late
Reoccupation

Sechin
River

0   50   100 m

▦ Platform
〰 Late Prehistoric Canal
- - - Hill

N

Fig. 50. View from the southwest of the main structure at Huerequeque, showing the built-up nature of the rectangular and circular courts.

sherds we encountered were a single example each of zoned graphite and combed appliqué bumps.

On the basis of architecture and ceramics, Huerequeque clearly belongs chronologically within the Initial Period development of the Casma Valley. The architectural configuration of the main mound associated with successive square and circular courts is much like the mound-plaza-circle layout of the northeastern part of Huaca A of Pampa de las Llamas-Moxeke. Ceramically, the use of graphite and plastic decoration such as combed appliqué bumps has been documented for the Initial Period occupation of Las Haldas immediately prior to the construction of the now-visible temple. Because of these similarities with both Pampa de las Llamas-Moxeke and Las Haldas, Huerequeque is tentatively assigned to a span of time which overlaps with the period of occupation of both of these more intensively studied sites.

Fig. 49. Plan of Huerequeque showing the main structure with its associated rectangular and circular courts surrounded by terraces containing domestic structures. Later canals cut through the site and watered some agricultural terraces at the south end of the site.

PALLKA

The site of Pallka is located about 35 kilometers inland at an elevation of about 900 meters on the south side of the Matwa tributary of the Casma branch of the river (fig. 2). Its situation affords an excellent view of the junction of the Río Yautan and the Río Grande valleys. Tello (1956: 32–43) surveyed it in 1937 with the aid of Collier, but there is no record of further work at the site prior to our surveys there in 1978 and 1980.

Pallka consists of two areas of architecture (fig. 51). The better-known complex containing the main mound covers about 110 meters by 220 meters on a leveled and reinforced river terrace well above the valley floor. It includes a relatively small (80 by 50 meters) but high (15 meters) mound of angular stones set in mud mortar associated with both rectangular and circular courts or plazas (fig. 52). In contrast to examples such as Sechin Alto which have a distinctly linear arrangement, the plazas of Pallka are not in line with the central mound axis.

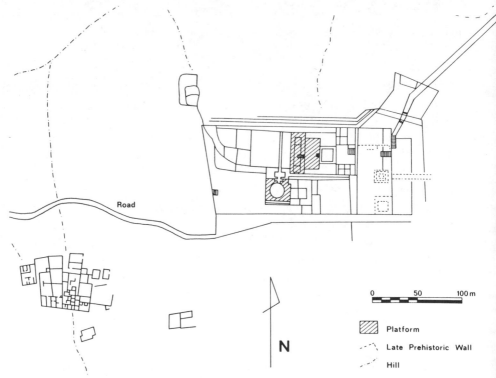

Fig. 51. Plan of Pallka showing the main mound, associated rooms and sunken circular court, and a small domestic area to the west.

Fig. 52. General view from the south showing the main mound of Pallka and its associated rooms and sunken court.

The circular court, which Williams (1972: 6) first described working from air photographs, is alongside and slightly behind the main mound. It was formed within a raised platform, and piles of earth and stone which obscure architecture immediately to the east of the circle may be a by-product of its construction. One associated road runs along the hillside immediately south of the main mound complex and borders on the southern plazas. A second road descends from the northeast corner of the main mound complex into the valley below. Until it enters the limits of cultivation, the road course is clearly distinguishable because of partial walls built of the cleared stones and occasional steps cut into the hillside.

The second area of architecture is a set of what appear to be domestic structures higher on the hill, about 150 meters southwest of the main mound (fig. 51). In consists of series of contiguous rooms with low walls of angular cobbles and boulders. Associated midden areas contain abundant ceramics as well as food remains. Northwest of the main mound area, Tello (1956: 35) located a badly looted cemetery area which yielded fragments of early as well as much later pottery.

There is additional evidence of a much later prehistoric occupation in the vicinity of the main mound. Southeast of this structure is a pair of small pyramidal mounds made of very flat, rectangular, cane-marked adobes, and several low walls nearby are formed of the same material. Ceramics in this zone suggest a Late Intermediate Period date for these constructions, which clearly postdate the main occupation of the site. A road, described by Tello (1956: 34), emanating from the more northern of the two structures appears to be of the same late date.

Pallka is renowed for its ceramics, which Tello (1956: 36–47) describes as "Chavin." Our survey yielded ceramics (fig. 53) similar to those Tello had illustrated. Both fineware and utilitarian vessels are represented, and a wide range of forms is present, including neckless ollas, short-necked jars, tall-necked bottles, bottles with thick stirrup spouts, pan-pipes, and shallow and deep bowls. Decorative techniques are even more varied and consist of incision, punctation, combing, rocker stamping, fabric impressions on vessel exteriors, and surface coloring with graphite. Many of these designs serve to tie Pallka chronologically with better-known sites nearer the coast. Combed bumps and the use of graphite connect the site with Huerequeque and Las Haldas, and the use of zoned punctation suggests additional ties between Pallka and Las

Fig. 53. Ceramics and artifacts collected from the surface of both the mound complex and domestic area of Pallka. The variety of ceramic decoration and form indicates connections with both the coast and the highlands.

Haldas. Other elements, however, reveal connections with later lower-valley sites. These include the thick stirrup spout, thick flaring rim, and panpipe vessel forms, as well as decorative elements such as circle-and-dot motifs and fabric impressions along with a slate blade fragment. Other features such as stamped decoration and elaborate curvilinear incised designs are distinct from features of collections nearer the coast and undoubtedly reflect Pallka's location, which affords access to sierra as well as coastal influences.

Since Tello's time, additional data from excavated sites in the lower Casma Valley make it possible to assess the occupation of Pallka. Ceramic similarities to Huerequeque and especially to the more reliably dated site of Las Haldas argue for an occupation of Pallka which clearly predates the Chavin development during the Early Horizon. To some extent the form of the Pallka main mound and the presence of a circular court comprise ties with early coastal sites; but important differences, such as the location of the circular court, suggest that Pallka was far enough removed and/or sufficiently affected by nearby highland influences to prevent strict adherence to coastal architectural tenets. Elements of Pallka's ceramic inventory which tie it securely to later coastal sites provide evidence of a long local occupation, but there is no surface evidence of architectural modifications associated with this later phase of the occupation. In sum, Pallka is especially important because its occupation spans a time period which saw two very distinctive occupations in the lower valley.

HUACA DESVIO

Huaca Desvio is located about 32 kilometers inland and approximately 720 meters above sea level on the north side of the Sechin branch of the river (fig. 2). Fung and Williams (1977: 123, 126) have grouped together three substantial mounds as well as associated smaller structures (fig. 54) under this designation. One mound of stone construction lies above the cultivated valley bottom on an ancient river terrace. It is associated with an oval court located in front of the mound and is generally aligned with the magnetic E26°N orientation of the central mound axis. A second mound, created of stone set in mud mortar, lies about 600 meters west of the mound/oval court complex on a lower terrace of the Sechin River, just outside modern cultivation. Its orientation varies almost 90° from the first mound, and it is U-shaped with the entrance toward the south. Construction of this mound clearly took advantage of the sloping

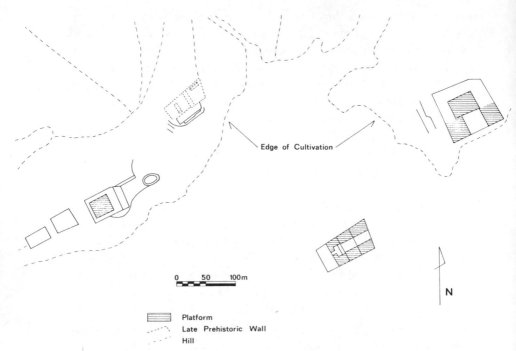

Edge of Cultivation

0   50   100m

N

Platform
Late Prehistoric Wall
Hill

Fig. 54. Plan of Huaca Desvio, which mainly consists of three mounds and an oval sunken court.

hillside—the north portions of both wings are outlined but not significantly built up. A third mound of similar construction materials lies between and south of the other two examples and within the limits of modern cultivation. It has a distinctive U shape with definite wings, and its magnetic orientation of E23°N is close to that of the mound-and-court complex to the northwest.

There is evidence of later, probably Late Intermediate Period, reoccupation of all three mounds. This is most pronounced on the upper river terrace, where earlier artificial terraces have clearly been remodeled using rectangular adobes. Much of the surrounding hillside is covered with agricultural terraces associated with late ceramics, and these same ceramic types occur on the early mounds.

Early ceramics associated with the three mounds serve to correlate Huaca Desvio with the sites of Pampa Rosario and San Diego in the lower valley and with Pallka in the upper Casma drainage. Important features of the Huaca Desvio ceramic inventory include vessel forms of panpipes, flaring-rim jars, tall-neck jars, and grater bowls, and decoration using circle-and-dot motifs (fig. 55), interior fabric impressions,

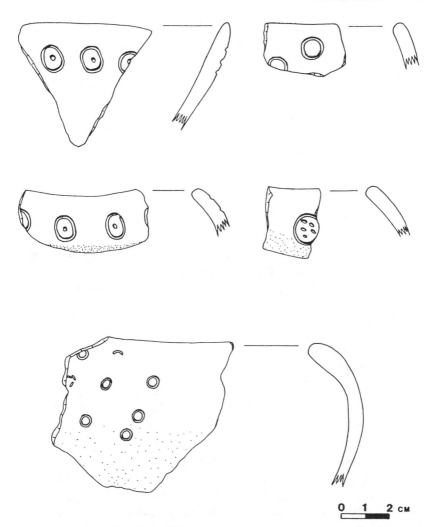

Fig. 55. Ceramics from the site of Huaca Desvio showing representative circle-and-dot designs as well as the vessel forms upon which they occur.

and white paint as well as incision and zoned punctation. The circle-and-dot motif seems much more abundant on ceramics at Huaca Desvio than in collections from the lower-valley sites, a factor which correlates well with recent data on sites in the upper Nepeña Valley immediately to the north, where the circle-and-dot motif is even more common (R. Daggett 1984: 187; Proulx 1985). We explore these correlations more fully in the concluding chapter.

Some of the less common decorative techniques such as zoned punctation, as well as the architectural presence of U-shaped mounds and a mound aligned with a roughly circular court, provide suggestions of an earlier occupation than most of the ceramics indicate. Fung and Williams (1977: 134) note architectural similarities between Huaca Desvio and Sechin Alto, but date the main Huaca Desvio occupation considerably later on the basis of ceramics. Thus it appears that Huaca Desvio, like Pallka, may span the time represented by more than one major phase of lower-valley occupation. Still, it is possible that the considerable deviance from coastal architectural tenets at both upvalley sites reflects spatial as well as chronological differences.

LA CANTINA

La Cantina is located in a small quebrada on the south side of the Casma branch of the Casma Valley, at an elevation of 130 meters and some 14 kilometers inland from the Pacific Ocean (fig. 2). Tello (1956: 72–74) first reported on the site, calling it a Chavin temple. His schematic plan of the site (Tello 1956: fig. 35) is somewhat inaccurate, but generally shows the site's approximate layout and dimensions. Thompson (1961: 83–84, 256–259, 1962a: 294–295, 1964a: 209) dates the site to the Late Formative, 400 B.C. to 0 B.C./A.D., based mainly on ceramics found there and secondarily on architectural form. Our survey evidence generally agrees with Thompson's dating of the site.

La Cantina measures about 420 meters northeast-southwest by 230 meters northwest-southeast (fig. 56). Its main-axis magnetic orientation is N41°E, the same orientation as Pampa de las Llamas-Moxeke, which is situated across the valley from La Cantina. The site consists of a small rectangular platform mound associated with three plazas of increasing size as one ventures northwest away from the mound (fig. 57). The platform mound, the two plazas nearest it, and about one-fourth of the outermost plaza are enclosed within a large rectangular compound

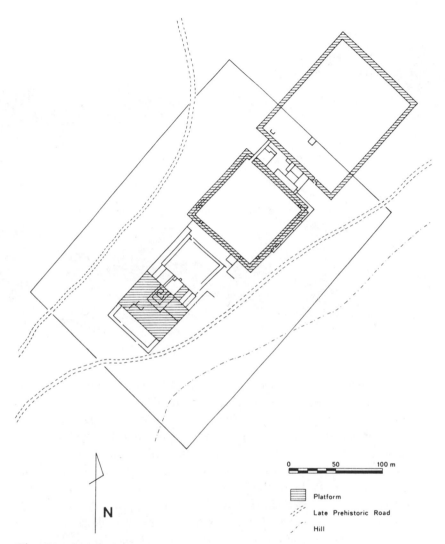

N

0   50   100 m

Platform

Late Prehistoric Road

Hill

Fig. 56. Plan of La Cantina, which has a principal mound and three main plazas, most of which are enclosed by a large compound.

Fig. 57. General view of La Cantina from the southeast.

that maintains its symmetry even in its southern corner, which rests on a steep hillside. The remainder of the outermost plaza lies 2 to 3 meters below the rest of the site and is largely obscured by the heavy looting of a Late Intermediate Period cemetery in the same area. The middle plaza is separated from the outermost plaza by a series of low-walled rooms, and passage between the plazas is by means of a central staircase. This middle plaza is notable for the presence of eight paired entrance ramps or staircases, two on each side of the plaza. Also noteworthy is the presence of two terrace or bench levels which define the plaza sides: the lower inner bench is composed of distinctive dark basaltic rock which contrasts with the lighter gray rock of the higher outer bench. The plaza closest to the platform mound is somewhat irregular, possibly because of different construction phases or alternative access routes from the southeast that bypass the other two plazas. The platform mound is badly looted, and only remnants of wall patterns remain. Immediately behind the main platform mound is a small plaza or large room defined by a pair of walls with nonaligned entrances.

Most of the construction material is quarried stone set in silty clay mortar. Our observations confirm those of Tello (1956: 74), however, that part of the platform mound contains rectangular, conical, and possibly odontoform adobes, though the latter are badly eroded and their true form may be obscured.

We recovered relatively few ceramics from the site, but we found enough to establish the site as partially contemporary with San Diego, Pampa Rosario, Huaca Desvio, and Pallka and more completely contemporary with Chankillo. The vessel forms we found include neckless ollas, short-neck jars, panpipes, and widely flaring jars, somewhat like flaring Salinar rims found in valleys farther north. The ceramic decoration includes circle-and-dot designs, exterior fabric impressions, and zoned punctations. Perforated sherd disks are also present.

CHANKILLO

The site of Chankillo is located about 15 kilometers from the Pacific Ocean on the south side of the Casma branch of the Casma Valley (fig. 2). The area described here as Chankillo contains, in addition to the famous hilltop fortress, the enigmatic Thirteen Steps or Towers, three sets of compounds, and extensive midden areas (fig. 58). The hilltop fortress stands about 300 meters above sea level, whereas the remainder of the site is at an elevation of 175 meters. The site components are generally treated separately when mentioned in the literature, but we have grouped them together in this study on the basis of similarities in both masonry construction and ceramic evidence.

The hilltop fortress, variously referred to as Chankillo, Chanquillo, Chancayillo, or Chancaillo, is one of the most frequently described sites of the Casma Valley (Fung and Pimentel 1973; Kroeber 1944: 52–53; Kosok 1965: 211, 213; Middendorf 1973a: 214–219, 222; Roosevelt 1935: 26; Squier 1877: 211–212; Tello 1956: 68–71; Thompson 1961: 262–265, 1964a: 209–210). Squier visited the site in the 1860s and produced an excellent plan of the fortress (Squier 1877: 211–212), which Middendorf (1973a: 214) and Kosok (1965: 211) subsequently reproduced. The fortress is constructed of angular granite cobbles and boulders aligned to present a relatively smooth face, with interstices filled by spall chinking. The plan of the fortress consists of three generally concentric oval walls with five, four, and three entrances, respectively. These walls encircle one rectangular and two circular structures (fig. 59); they stand about 3 to 6 meters high and decrease in thickness from outside in, ranging from about 4 meters to less than 2.5 meters thick. Both Squier (1877: 211) and

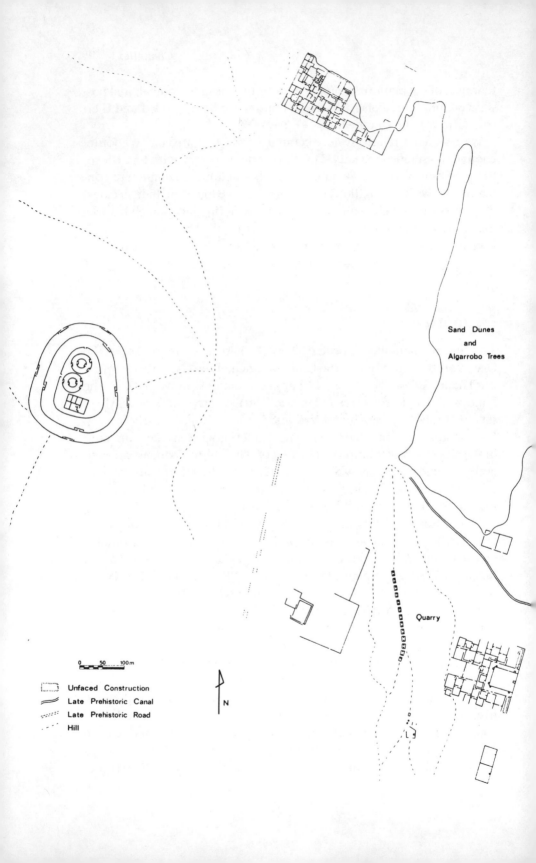

Sand Dunes
and
Algarrobo Trees

Quarry

0   50   100 m

░ Unfaced Construction
═ Late Prehistoric Canal
⋯ Late Prehistoric Road
· Hill

N

Fig. 59. General view from the northwest of the Chankillo fortress.

Tello (1956: 68–69) have described the internal wall construction, which consists of multiple parallel wall faces as well as fill. Middendorf (1973a: 215) describes remnants of parapets still visible on the outermost wall when he visited the site in the 1880s. Fung and Pimentel (1973: figs. 1–3) illustrate inset staircases on either side of the gates to the outer wall; these afforded access to the wall tops behind the parapet. We observed additional inset stairways at regular intervals along the entire outer wall. Traces of yellow plaster containing coarse sand on many protected wall faces suggest that the entire structure was similarly treated. Fung and Pimentel (1973: 72) encountered an additional cap of fine yellow clay in areas they excavated, so this surface treatment may also have been omnipresent at the site.

The entrances penetrating the three outer walls and the innermost pair of circles have successively different systems of baffles and interior staircases, which have been described in detail (Fung and Pimentel 1973: figs. 1–2; Squier 1877: 211; Thompson 1961: 264). All apparently had *al-garrobo* (*Prosopis chilensis*) wood lintels, and Fung and Pimentel sug-

Fig. 58. Plan of Chankillo showing the fortress, Thirteen Steps, two large, symmetrical multiroom compounds, and other associated architecture.

gest that wooden doors were also present. They illustrate remains of paired latches on either side of entrances in the outermost and second encircling walls (Fung and Pimentel 1973: photos 2, 3, 5). In the interior passageways of these gates and other protected areas, Squier (1877: 212) observed "traces of figures in relief, paintings of men and animals, and what are apparently battle-scenes." Comparable drawings encountered by Fung and Pimentel in 1967 when they cleared a passageway depict late, probably Late Intermediate Period, motifs (Fung and Pimentel 1973: 76, photos 6–10). All apparently represent graffiti or vandalism of the site by later prehistoric peoples.

Squier (1877: 211–212) observed that the hillslope behind all the encircling walls had been filled in to some extent, but this artificial alteration of the hill surface was greatest behind the innermost of the three walls. This fill serves to level the hilltop beneath the round and rectangular structures. The two double-walled round structures were also entered via baffled entrances. Excavations in one by Thompson (1961: 264) revealed a floor of yellow adobe plaster overlying leveled flagstones. Thompson also observed evidence of later reuse of this structure, something that is confirmed by our observations of late burials which had recently been looted. A rectangular compound of seven rooms is the third structure enclosed by the encircling walls. Significantly, access to this compound is gained on the southeast side by means of two paired ramps or staircases, set in either end of a low platform with summit columns similar to examples found at San Diego and Pampa Rosario.

Collier (1962: 413) reports a radiocarbon date of 342 ± 80 B.C. (Olson and Broecker 1959: 32) from a wooden lintel, and Henri Reichlen secured a second date of 120 ± 100 B.C., also on a lintel (Radiocarbon Dates Association, Inc., n.d.). However, excavations by Fung and Pimentel (1973: 77) yielded no sherds, and surface reconnaissance resulted only in collections of late ceramics probably associated with the intrusive architecture and burials (Kroeber 1944: 52). Middendorf felt the structure was not continuously used because no wear was visible on the exposed stone steps; this lack of wear also explained the paucity of ceramics (Middendorf 1973a: 215–216).

On the ridge of a low hill 750 meters to the east of the fortress is a series of Thirteen Steps or Towers (fig. 60) which have also been frequently discussed (Kosok 1965: 213; Kroeber 1944: 52; Middendorf 1973a: 216–217; Roosevelt 1935: 26; Thompson 1961: 269–271). Thompson (1961: 269–271) best described the structures, which consist of solid, angular stone masonry with spall chinking that closely resembles the fortress

Fig. 60. General view of the Thirteen Steps from the compound to the east at the foot of the hill.

masonry. The structures extend north-south along the hillcrest, with number 11 (from the north) at the summit. Their varied heights reflect a not entirely successful attempt to make the level of their tops approximately the same. Number 11 is only 2 meters high, whereas number 1 is 5.8 meters high. Each tower is approximately 11 by 8 meters in area, and they average about 3 meters apart. On both the north and south faces of the northern twelve are inset staircases (fig. 61), but the southernmost tower has an inset staircase only within its north face. Virtually all investigators who attempt to interpret this enigmatic architectural form assign a ceremonial or calendrical function to the Thirteen Steps. Middendorf (1973a: 219) wondered if they might be altars, and attempted to correlate his miscounted number of twelve towers with the solar calendar. Roosevelt (1935: 26) postulated their function as altars or beacons and connected the number 13 with the lunar calendar, a calendrical interpretation also favored by Kosok (1965: 213).

On the plain between the fortress and the Thirteen Steps is a series of compounds (fig. 58) Thompson described as a probable residential site (Thompson 1961: 266–267, 1964a: 210). Remains of two walled compounds and two courts are present, and the outstanding feature is the east wall of one compound, which still stands about 7 meters high. The absence of the remainder of the compound, given such high walls, sug-

Fig. 61. Detail of a set of steps within one of the structures of the Thirteen Steps.

gests that either the structure was never completed, or, more likely, that the stones have since been robbed for use elsewhere. The area east of the structures at the base of the hill is protected from fierce local winds and yielded abundant surface remains of shell and early ceramics.

On the plain east of the ridge with the Thirteen Steps is a large compound of the same angular granite masonry as the structures farther west. The symmetrical compound, which measures about 160 meters by 170 meters, contains a U-shaped series of rooms around a sunken rectangular court (fig. 62). Thompson remarked on the compound's labyrinthine configuration of twenty-seven closed rooms and eight partially open and possibly unfinished peripheral rooms, all interconnected by baffled doorways (Thompson 1961: 272, 1964a: 210). Roosevelt felt the ceramics from this "residential site" were the key to dating the more mysterious nearby ruins (Roosevelt 1935: 27). We found surface sherds associated with the rooms.

North and south of the labyrinthine compound are other compounds of similar construction and materials which are less elaborate. On air photographs and in figure 62, a series of sunken rectangular courts aligned with the ornate compound is faintly visible extending at least

1500 meters toward the east (not shown in fig. 58). Surface examination of these features revealed close similarities to the sunken court within the compound. However, examples far to the east were cut into the sandy pampa, but were unfaced and therefore difficult to detect. Also in this zone, west and south of the labyrinthine compound, surface concentrations of marine shells define extensive midden areas which average an estimated 50 centimeters to 1 meter deep and cover approximately 24 hectares near the compounds and sunken courts.

North of the fortress and near the edge of cultivation in an area of the plain badly inundated by eolian sand is a second multiroom compound (fig. 58). The portion not covered by sand or *algarrobo* trees measures 250 meters by 130 meters, so this compound was probably much larger than the examples nearer the Thirteen Steps. Although only the southern portion of this compound is visible, the internal layout suggests that the compound's form may have been very similar to that of the smaller ornate compound. They share a similar orientation, and the remnant of the north compound consists of small labyrinthine rooms with baffled doorways, possibly arranged around a larger central room and forming a

Fig. 62. General view of the compound to the east of the Thirteen Steps. Large rectangular plazas are visible in the background.

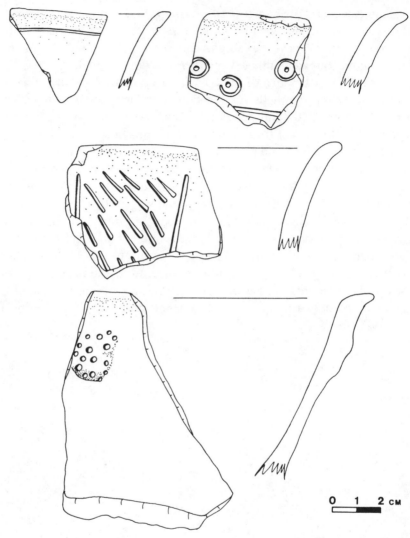

Fig. 63. Tall-neck jar rims from surface collections at Chankillo that exhibit a variety of exterior decoration techniques.

U shape around a large court toward the south. Assuming symmetry, the postulated original dimensions for the compound are approximately 250 meters by 200 meters. Incorporated with the stone construction of the compound are numerous large trapezoidal adobes, unlike any seen at other sites within the Casma Valley. We recorded wind-deflated zones of shallow midden at the base of the hill south of this compound, and this surface as well as some of the rooms yielded early ceramics.

Most of the ceramics from the Chankillo zone come from the west base of the ridge with the Thirteen Steps and especially from the main compound and midden areas east of this hill. Vessel forms which include panpipes, short-neck and tall-neck jars, flaring-rim jars, and neckless ollas provide evidence of chronological overlap with the occupations of San Diego and Pampa Rosario. Decorative techniques and motifs of exterior fabric impression, slash punctations, and circle-and-dot designs, as well as the presence of many shaped and drilled sherd disks, further reinforce these ties. One notable difference between the ceramics at Chankillo and those of San Diego and Pampa Rosario is the abundance of tall-neck jar rims at Chankillo which are frequently decorated on the exterior (fig. 63). The change in frequency of this ceramic trait may reflect a slightly longer duration of occupation at Chankillo than at either San Diego or Pampa Rosario. Although no ceramics are available from the fortress, its radiocarbon dates and the paired-ramp system which link it to Pampa Rosario and San Diego place Chankillo within the range of our study. These data correlate very well with the independent ceramic evidence from the rest of the site, and, taken together, they indicate that Chankillo is one of the latest sites we investigated.

4

The Prehistory of the Casma Valley and Its Impact on Studies of Early Andean Prehistory

In this chapter, we use the excavation and survey data presented in chapters 2 and 3 to create a revised chronological sequence for major Cotton Preceramic, Initial Period, and Early Horizon sites in the Casma Valley area (table 1). In order to put our work in perspective, we devote the first section to a review of chronological sequences proposed by previous investigators in the area. This includes an assessment of the evidence upon which these sequences were based.

New excavation data from sites which had previously been untested or briefly tested, along with over thirty radiocarbon dates from these sites, were critical to the formulation of this new sequence. However, architectural and artifactual data were also important, especially for unexcavated sites. We use these data, taken together, to reconstruct early prehistoric ways of life in the Casma Valley for the late Cotton Preceramic through the Early Horizon. We also attempt to put these developments in perspective through brief comparisons with other areas.

Our new sequence reveals that most of the significant early developments within the Casma Valley occurred during the Initial Period and *before* the Early Horizon. This means that they could neither be associated with nor influenced by the Chavin phenomenon. Instead, it appears increasingly likely that Initial Period sites in the Casma Valley and elsewhere along the north and central coast influenced Chavin de Huantar, the best-known locus of the Chavin phenomenon. As more of the truly spectacular developments are attributed to the Initial Period, the Casma data assume even greater importance because there is so little information from sites which are securely dated to the Early Horizon. We discuss the evidence for and implications of all these developments in the final segment of this chapter.

PREVIOUS SEQUENCES FOR CASMA VALLEY PREHISTORY

Previous investigators, as early as Middendorf in the late 1800s, have tried, in their interpretations of early Casma Valley prehistory, to relate the sites to the Chavin phenomenon. Middendorf (1973a: 219–223, 1973b: 81) first proposed that Moxeke had been constructed by an ancient state or empire that included the Santa and Nepeña Valleys; the center of this empire was possibly the site of Chavin de Huantar. He based this hypothesis on his idea that Casma was too small and underdeveloped a valley to have supported a population large enough to build large mounds such as Moxeke. He reasoned that the empire had been both pre-Inca and pre-Chimu, since Cieza de Leon (1973: 174–176) did not even mention the valley in his chronicles and since Moxeke and similar mounds did not resemble any Chimu architecture that he had seen. Finally, Middendorf proposed that the Recuay pottery style, the earliest highland style yet identified, was typical of this early empire.

In 1934, Julio C. Tello briefly visited the Casma Valley during a trip along the coast and into the highlands in the company of Cornelius Van S. Roosevelt (1935). Inspired by this trip, Tello, accompanied by Mejia Xesspe, Collier, and other assistants, returned to the Casma Valley in 1937 and carried out the first scientific exploration and excavations there (Tello 1943, 1956). During this time Tello recognized that Casma contained a great number of early ceramic sites—sites which he attributed to the Chavin culture. Casma sites he recognized as early and called "Chavin" include Pallka, Pampa de las Llamas, Moxeke, Chankillo, La Cantina, Taukachi-Konkan, Sechin Alto, and Cerro Sechin (Tello 1956: 10–11, 32–83). Except for Cerro Sechin, Tello made no chronological differentiation among these mounds. He assigned Cerro Sechin to his second period of Chavin culture, called Sub-Chavin (Tello 1956: 278–280). Tello also explored San Diego but was misled by surrounding looted late cemeteries, calling it Sub-Chimu and dating it to the Late Intermediate Period (Tello 1956: 296–298).

Tello's investigations were marred by inadequate associations of recognizable ceramics with architecture, stone carvings, and adobe friezes. This is a critical problem both because early sites often contain very few surface sherds and because many early sites were prehistorically reoccupied and their mounds used for later burials. The only site from which Tello recovered abundant "Chavin" sherds was Pallka. At one point, Tello (1956: 82–83) states that he found no classic Chavin ceramics in the lower Casma Valley because these deposits were buried; however, in another section Tello (1956: 52) reports some Chavin-style ceramics from a looter's pit at Huaca A of Pampa de las Llamas. In either case, he found almost no "classic Chavin" sherds downvalley from the site of Pallka. Therefore his dating relied heavily on architectural form and construction technique, traits which were, and still are, essential criteria for evaluating early coastal sites in general. For Tello (1956: 60–66, 84–288), the additional indications of the presence of the Chavin culture in Casma are the adobe friezes at Moxeke and the carved monoliths at Cerro Sechin, neither of which had clear ceramic associations when he excavated them.

Collier (1962) and Thompson (1961, 1962a, 1964a) conducted a more systematic survey of the valley in 1956 and briefly tested five sites: Sechin Alto, Chankillo, Pampa Rosario, Pampa de las Llamas, and Cerro Sechin. On the basis of this survey and excavation data, Collier (1962: 411–414) identified late Cotton Preceramic sites on the bays of Tortugas and Huaynuná which Engel (1957a: 56, 1957b: 74–75) subsequently tested. He also proposed a sequence of three ceramic styles during the Formative Period: Cahuacucho (Early Formative, 1200 to 750 B.C.), Gualaño (Middle Formative, 750 to 400 B.C.), and Patazca (Late Formative, 400 B.C. to 0 B.C./A.D.). The first two ceramic styles were recovered only from test excavations at Sechin Alto (Collier 1962: 411), whereas the later Patazca style ceramics were noted in surface collections from the Moxeke mound, Chankillo, Sechin Alto, and in test excavations at Pampa Rosario. There is some question as to the validity of the stratigraphic relationship between Cahuacucho and Gualaño pottery, especially in view of the inverted radiocarbon and thermoluminescent dates (Bueno and Samaniego 1969: 34; Fung 1969: 186). Although Patazca pottery was not found stratigraphically overlying either Cahuacucho or Gualaño pottery (Collier 1962: 412), there seems little reason to doubt that these two styles predate Patazca pottery and its associated types. Collier (1962: 412–414) has correlated Gualaño and Patazca pottery with the Viru Valley sequence, and our evidence from Casma supports the general ordering of the Cahuacucho and Gualaño styles before Patazca. Until more concrete evidence is found, however, we would group Cahuacucho and Gualaño together because the difference between them seems to be undecorated versus decorated pottery.

The definition of the Patazca style is based primarily on excavated ceramic samples from Pampa Rosario, so it contains most of the associated ceramic traits which we have documented for both Pampa Rosario and San Diego. However, the Patazca style also includes elements defined on the basis of survey collections from sites with multiple components, and therefore may not overlap exactly with the definition of our late style. Our radiocarbon dates indicate that this style probably does not date as late as Collier suggests, but instead begins a few hundred years earlier and ends about 200 B.C. A key point of discrepancy is the presence of Patazca pottery on the top of Moxeke recorded by Collier and Thompson. This pottery probably reflects a later reuse of the zone because our excavation data indicate that the main occupation of Pampa de las Llamas-Moxeke occurred much earlier than the Late Formative time span proposed by Collier and Thompson. Collier (1962: 414) does note that the pottery at the Chankillo fortress and the associated compound near the Thirteen Steps is slightly different. This coincides with our observations and with radiocarbon dates of 120 ± 100 B.C. and 342 ± 80 B.C. from wooden lintels in the fortress (Olson and Broecker 1959: 22; Radiocarbon Dates Association, Inc., n.d.).

On the basis of the same survey and using both architectural patterns and ceramics, Thompson (1961, 1962a, 1964a, 1974) proposed more specific dating for many early Casma Valley sites (table 3). Utilizing the same periods as Collier—Early Formative, Middle Formative, and Late Formative—Thompson (1961: 63–97, 1962a: 293–297, 1964a: 206–211, 1974: 11–17) reconstructs the sequence of early sites as follows. Sechin Alto, and perhaps some other large mounds, was probably started in the Early Formative. During the Middle Formative, Pallka, Moxeke, the main part of Sechin Alto, Pampa Rosario (Thompson's several sites numbered C17–C20), San Diego, and Cerro Sechin were constructed. Taukachi-Konkan is equivocably either late Middle Formative or early Late Formative. La Cantina, Sechin Bajo, Huaca A of Pampa de las Llamas-Moxeke, and Chankillo and its associated structures were built in the Late Formative. Although Thompson did not recognize the presence of sunken circular forecourts at early Casma Valley sites, his use of other architectural patterns, techniques, and building materials (Thompson 1962a: 292) greatly increased his ability to chronologically place sites which yielded few or no sherds or where obvious late intrusive sherds masked the true date of original site construction. His sequence differs from Collier's in that he places the sites with Patazca pottery mainly in the Middle rather than the Late Formative. Although we disagree with the late dating of specific sites such as Huaca A of Pampa

TABLE 3. A Comparison of Casma Valley Chronological Sequences

	Thompson		Fung & Williams		Pozorski & Pozorski, This Volume	
	Sequence	Chronological Placement of Sites	Sequence	Chronological Placement of Sites	Sequence	Chronological Placement of Sites
2500 B.C.						
2400 B.C.						
2300 B.C.						
2200 B.C.			Cotton Precer.		Cotton Precer.	
2100 B.C.						
2000 B.C.						
1900 B.C.						Huaynuná Precer. Las Haldas
1800 B.C.		Precer. Tortugas Huaynuná				
1700 B.C.						Las Haldas
1600 B.C.	Cotton Precer.					P. Llamas-Moxeke
1500 B.C.						Tortugas
						Sechin Alto

B.C.	Period		Period		Period	
	(Formative)		Early Horizon	Taukachi-Konkan	Early Horizon	
1300 B.C.						Huerequeque
1200 B.C.	Early Formative	Sechin Alto				Palka
1100 B.C.						Sechin Bajo
1000 B.C.						Taukachi-Konkan
900 B.C.				Sechin Alto / Taukachi-Konkan / Sechin Bajo / Huaca Desvio		Las Haldas
800 B.C.						Sechin Alto
700 B.C.	Middle Formative	Sechin Alto / Pallka / Moxeke / Pampa Rosario / San Diego / Cerro Sechin / -Taukachi-Konkan-		Sechin Alto / Sechin Bajo / Konkan / Huerequeque		Cerro Sechin
600 B.C.						Pallka
500 B.C.						Pampa Rosario
400 B.C.	Late Formative	La Cantina / P. Llamas-Huaca A / Chankillo / Sechin Bajo		Sechin Alto / Huaca Desvio / Sechin Bajo / Huerequeque		Huaca Desvio
300 B.C.						San Diego
200 B.C.						La Cantina
100 B.C.						Chankillo
B.C./A.D.						

de las Llamas-Moxeke and Sechin Bajo, Thompson's general placement of most mounds earlier in time was an important contribution. Thompson (1964a: 207) concludes, however, as does Collier (1962: 414), that Patazca pottery is derivative of Chavin-style pottery and that virtually all of the mounds in Casma are Chavin or later in date (Thompson 1961: 132–134, 1962a: 296–297, 1964a: 207–209).

Fung and Williams (1977: 111–156) have presented the only additional chronological sequence for early Casma Valley sites (table 3), concentrating on sites in the Sechin branch of the valley, where they performed a survey in 1968. They, like Thompson, rely on architectural characteristics as well as surface ceramics. Because air photographs had become available, some of the more obscure circular forecourts were more readily visible. Consequently, they are the first investigators to include sunken circular forecourts in their chronological scheme. Fung and Williams (1977: 144) date the sites pertinent to our study as follows. During the Initial Period, construction of Sechin Alto and Taukachi-Konkan was started. The isolated pyramidal mound was the main architectural form. In the early part of the Early Horizon, Sechin Bajo and Huaca Desvio were built and occupation of Sechin Alto and Taukachi-Konkan continued. Mounds associated with sunken circular forecourts formed the dominant architectural pattern. During the middle Early Horizon, Huerequeque was constructed, while occupation of Sechin Alto, Sechin Bajo, and the Konkan sector of Taukachi-Konkan continued. Pyramidal mounds with corridors and sunken circular forecourts were the main architectural mode. In the late Early Horizon, Sechin Alto continued to be occupied and was characterized by additional construction using conical adobes. Fung and Williams also discuss later occupations at Huaca Desvio, Sechin Bajo, and Huerequeque. This sequence they present is a significant contribution to the study of early Casma Valley prehistory; however, like Thompson and Collier, they refer to the Chavin culture as responsible for most of the major mound sites in the Sechin branch. Although they recognize the presence of sunken circular courts on the coast in the late Cotton Preceramic, they do not believe this feature was widely disseminated until the Chavin horizon (Fung and Williams 1977: 132), when its proliferation was associated with the arrival of local Chavin influence. This implies that relatively little transpired in the way of monumental construction during the entire Initial Period.

A REVISED SEQUENCE OF EVENTS IN CASMA VALLEY
PREHISTORY

On the basis of recent excavation and survey within the Casma Valley,
we propose a sequence which differs markedly from earlier assessments
of local prehistory (tables 1 and 3). Our new data, especially radiocarbon dates, suggest that the most significant developments in early Casma
Valley prehistory occurred well before the Early Horizon. The coastal
Cotton Preceramic Period sites near Casma are not so spectacular as
some more southern examples, but Huaynuná contains sizable mounds
which indicate labor expenditures for nonsubsistence-oriented pursuits
at the site. By the very early Initial Period, however, developments in
Casma were truly spectacular. Large mound sites 2 to over 10 square
kilometers in area had become established. Major architectural and
settlement pattern changes occurred during the Initial Period, and the
trend was always toward increasingly larger mound-dominated sites.
The architectural, ceramic, and subsistence evidence of the Early Horizon contrasts markedly with established patterns of the Initial Period.
This evidence reveals that early in the Early Horizon, or late in the Initial Period, drastic changes occurred within Casma—changes so drastic
that they appear attributable to outside invasion.

Late Cotton Preceramic

Recent fieldwork in the Casma Valley by Michael Malpass has documented the use of the valley by early preceramic populations (Malpass
1983). However, our reconstruction of early Casma Valley prehistory begins with the later portion of the Cotton Preceramic Period because it is
the time of the first permanent settlements. Within the Casma Valley
area, preceramic Las Haldas and Huaynuná are the main sites known to
date to this time period. Radiocarbon dates place both sites near the end
of the Cotton Preceramic Period, and both share many important features typical of the period.

Because of the overlying Initial Period component, the preceramic occupation of Las Haldas is not well known. Consisting of deep but not
dense midden, the site appears to have been large in extent, but it has
not yielded conclusive evidence of preceramic architecture. This is unusual, since most preceramic sites without architecture, such as Padre
Aban in the Moche Valley (S. Pozorski 1976, 1983) and sites near Ven-
tanilla Bay (Moseley 1975), are quite small.

Huaynuná more closely resembles the larger preceramic sites, which generally contain both domestic and nondomestic architecture. Such sites are fairly common along the northern and central coast. Examples include Alto Salaverry in the Moche Valley (S. Pozorski 1983; S. Pozorski and T. Pozorski 1979b), Salinas de Chao in the Chao Valley (Alva 1978: 275–276; Cardenas 1979: 20–22), Bandurria south of the Huaura Valley, Aspero in the Supe Valley (Feldman 1980, 1985; Moseley and Willey 1973), and El Paraíso in the Chillon Valley (Engel 1967; Quilter 1985). These sites are characterized by corporate-labor mounds which provide evidence of a work force devoted to nonsubsistence pursuits. Two sizable artificial mounds containing architecture have been tested at Huaynuná, and others probably exist within additional slightly raised areas at the site. The terraced hillside platform is certainly nondomestic and provides clear evidence of a local mound-building tradition that has roots in the Cotton Preceramic Period. Both preceramic Las Haldas and Huaynuná cover medium to large areas—a factor which suggests that a substantial local population existed by the end of the Cotton Preceramic.

Virtually all late Cotton Preceramic sites known are located in a coastal setting, and preceramic Las Haldas and Huaynuná are no exception. Some exceptions have been noted by Patterson (1971: 318), who has recorded small inland preceramic sites in the Chillon, Rimac, and Lurin Valleys. The coastal sites consistently comprise substantial settlements with deep and/or dense midden rich in the residues of marine resources. Clearly, proximity to this abundant and perennially available marine food supply was the key variable in late Cotton Preceramic site location, despite the fact that industrial and food plant species were cultivated and utilized. Consequently, preceramic coastal sites are often well away from river valleys and tend to be located in protected locations near good areas for fishing and collecting shellfish.

Both Huaynuná and preceramic Las Haldas fit this pattern, for both are nestled behind raised outcrops which afford protection from the wind and mist, and both are situated well away from the mouth of the Casma River. Similar adjacent sandy and rocky beaches were accessible to both sites, and their exploitation is reflected in faunal inventories which contain both rock- and sand-dwelling species. Differences between the molluscan inventories of the two sites may be due to variations in species distribution, a variable which has been documented in the Moche Valley (S. Pozorski 1976, 1983), or they may be due to differences in procurement methods. The latter is especially true for Huaynuná, where remains of *Choromytilus chorus* and *Argopecten pur-puratum* indicate that the inhabitants were regularly exploiting fairly deep-water habitats as well as the active tide zone. At both sites, individual shellfish are quite large, much larger on the average than modern examples, and this argues against the overexploitation of any species. Instead, the people of preceramic Las Haldas and Huaynuná were apparently harvesting a variety of locally available shellfish, and differences in species frequencies at the two sites are probably an indication of local preferences and availability rather than truly systematic exploitation focusing on a few species.

Cotton and gourd are the dominant cultigens at both sites, and this is in keeping with the local marine emphasis (S. Pozorski 1976; S. Pozorski and T. Pozorski 1979b). To fishermen without pottery, cotton lines and nets as well as gourd containers and floats were invaluable, hence the emphasis on these vital industrial plants. This pattern is consistent with data from other excavated late Cotton Preceramic Period sites (see Feldman 1980, 1985; Moseley 1975). The Huaynuná midden contains a greater variety of additional plants, but this may be because of the better preservation there than at preceramic Las Haldas. Important staples such as a variety of tubers and beans were already present, and the tubers may have been domesticated on the coast (Ugent et al. 1982, 1983). The range of preceramic cultigens, especially at Huaynuná, reveals that plant-tending practices were sufficiently advanced to deal with annuals as well as perennial field crops and fruit trees.

All these plants were most likely grown by cultivating seasonally flooded areas of the Casma River system which provided the nearest arable land. However, experimentation with irrigation by channeling this floodwater into small canals was also probably practiced at this time.

It is evident that two significant coastal preceramic sites grew up in the area, both dependent on the Casma Valley for plant cultigens from agricultural plots. Evidence from slightly later sites indicates that a high frequency of *nonusable* plant parts characterizes middens of sites whose occupants *actually engaged in agriculture* rather than receiving products by exchange. Abundant nonfiber cotton remains such as bolls at Huaynuná, therefore, suggest that the inhabitants of that coastal site periodically traveled to the valley to do their own floodwater farming. Marine resources were still of paramount importance, however, and this is reflected by the location of the sites, the emphasis on fishing gear, and the abundant physical residues of marine products.

Initial Period

The Initial Period in general was marked by the advent of irrigation agriculture accompanied by the introduction of both ceramics and the use of woven textiles. Perhaps most significant is irrigation agriculture, because it resulted in a shift in subsistence priorities from marine resources to cultivated plants. This change is reflected physically in a new settlement pattern which saw the major sites located inland, where canal irrigation was most easily practiced. These new inland sites are known from every coastal river valley from the Jequetepeque to the Lurin. Excavated examples include Limoncarro in the Jequetepeque Valley (T. Pozorski 1976), Huaca de los Reyes in the Moche Valley (T. Pozorski 1976, 1980, 1982), Cerro Blanco and Punkurí in the Nepeña Valley (Proulx 1973: 15, 18; Tello 1943: 136–139), Garagay in the Rimac Valley (Ravines 1975; Ravines and Isbell 1975), and Cardal in the Lurin Valley (Richard Burger, personal communication; Williams 1979–80: 99). These better-known Initial Period sites share certain characteristics, including one or more bilaterally symmetrical U-shaped mounds, which are substantially larger than preceramic examples; adornment of the mounds with monumental iconographic depictions; and orientation of the opening of the U upvalley, possibly because this is the direction of the water source (T. Pozorski 1976: 160; Williams 1985: 230). Each site appears to have been the capital of a small polity. Despite the greatly increased emphasis on agriculture, smaller—obviously subsidiary— coastal sites provided the still important marine resources (S. Pozorski and T. Pozorski 1979a). This new pattern of large inland sites and smaller coastal sites was reflected in the Initial Period development in the Casma Valley.

Our survey and excavation data indicate that Pampa de las Llamas-Moxeke, in the southern Casma branch of the river, and the Sechin Alto Complex, which includes Sechin Alto, Sechin Bajo, Taukachi-Konkan, and Cerro Sechin, in the northern Sechin branch, were established as part of the general Initial Period proliferation of inland sites. Both sets of sites are near arable land. Also in keeping with the general Initial Period patterns, Moxeke, the inner temples of Cerro Sechin, and Sechin Alto are known to be ornamented with friezes (Bonavia 1974: 29–42; Tello 1956: 60–66), and conical adobes were employed in the construction of each of these mounds. Huaca A of Pampa de las Llamas-Moxeke Sechin Bajo of the Sechin Alto Complex also share similarities. In contrast to their U-shaped counterparts, both contain numerous regularly laid out summit rooms bisected by a central "corridor" of lower rooms. These characteristics suggest that both may have served secular functions within their respective site complexes.

The clear presence of at least two adobe construction phases at Cerro Sechin plus the adobe core exposed by looters at Sechin Alto indicate that during the Initial Period these structures may have grown in stages. However, several dates for Pampa de las Llamas-Moxeke and Sechin Alto place the existence of both sites early in the Initial Period, and the numerous Pampa de las Llamas-Moxeke dates indicate that it continued to be occupied for most of the Initial Period. Since Huaca A appears complete, whereas its Sechin Alto Complex counterpart of Sechin Bajo is clearly under construction, there is some evidence that the Casma branch site had developed slightly more rapidly. However, portions of Pampa de las Llamas-Moxeke are also unfinished.

The coastal sites of Las Haldas and Tortugas were also occupied during the Initial Period. Chronological placement of Las Haldas is based on numerous radiocarbon dates, whereas the dating of Tortugas relies on artifactual similarities with the well-dated site of Pampa de las Llamas-Moxeke.

For the Initial Period, our excavation data come from the sites of Pampa de las Llamas-Moxeke, Tortugas, and Las Haldas. Largely on the basis of these data, it appears that distinct but contemporary political units were functioning within the two branches of the Casma Valley during the Initial Period—one centered at Pampa de las Llamas-Moxeke and the second having the Sechin Alto Complex as its capital.

Coincident ceramics, stone bowls, and twined textiles at Pampa de las Llamas-Moxeke and Tortugas verify their contemporaneity and close association. The floral and faunal inventories at these two sites are also very similar, suggesting that an exchange system of the type documented for the Moche Valley (S. Pozorski and T. Pozorski 1979a) was in operation between Pampa de las Llamas-Moxeke and Tortugas. Peanuts, avocado, and *cansaboca* are securely identified for the first time, and there is a concomitant quantitative increase in food-plant remains which can be attributed to the greater success of irrigation agriculture in Initial Period times. Additional evidence points to Pampa de las Llamas-Moxeke as the agricultural producer of the pair. At Pampa de las Llamas-Moxeke, many nonusable plant parts such as bean pods and especially cotton boll fragments occur in the middens, whereas at Tortugas such remains do not occur. Beans, for example, are represented at Tortugas almost exclusively by seeds, suggesting that the coastal people received already-shelled beans from the inland source. Conversely, for the earlier preceramic site of Huaynuná, we viewed the presence of non-usable plant parts in the coastal midden as evidence that the site's inhabitants were doing their own farming.

The Sechin Alto Complex and the Las Haldas Initial Period occupation probably shared a symbiotic relationship which resembled that of Pampa de las Llamas-Moxeke and Tortugas. Excavated data from this second system come from the Las Haldas refuse. The coastal midden there contains abundant evidence of the same range of cultigens known from the other two excavated Initial Period Casma Valley sites. Cotton boll fragments and other nonusable plant parts are relatively rare, thus providing evidence that Las Haldas was indeed part of an exchange system. However, the artifact inventory of Las Haldas argues *against* its close association with the Pampa de las Llamas-Moxeke/Tortugas system. Las Haldas Initial Period ceramics are distinctive and resemble examples from the surface collections at Sechin Alto, thereby establishing a possible connection with the inland Sechin Alto Complex. The architectural layout of Las Haldas, with its successive aligned plazas, one of which contains a circular forecourt, also argues for its association with the Sechin Alto Complex mounds, especially Sechin Alto. Available radiocarbon dates indicate that there were two separate symbiotic systems. Carbon-14 assays for Pampa de las Llamas-Moxeke and Las Haldas are especially numerous and coincidental, thereby documenting the sites' contemporaneity despite variations in architecture and especially artifacts. It appears that two independent polities existed in fairly close proximity, and they may have complemented each other in the manner of moieties. This is especially interesting since their "paths" must have crossed as goods moved north from Pampa de las Llamas-Moxeke to Tortugas and south from the Sechin Alto Complex to Las Haldas.

The inland hillside site of Huerequeque in the Sechin branch was also probably occupied during the Initial Period, and it may represent a continuation of the inland movement of major sites initiated by the establishment of Pampa de las Llamas-Moxeke and the Sechin Alto Complex. Its mound-plaza-circle architectural form and surrounding domestic units are reminiscent of the northeastern part of Pampa de las Llamas-Moxeke. However, ceramic traits tie Huerequeque with the Initial Period occupation of Las Haldas and by extension with the Sechin Alto Complex. This may suggest that Huerequeque was part of and/or influenced by the Sechin branch polity.

Architectural and especially ceramic evidence suggests that Pallka may have been established well inland on the Casma branch of the river at this time. Like Huerequeque, Pallka may represent a continuation of the inland movement of coastal sites, but the location of Pallka at the convergence of two major tributaries probably also indicates an appreciation of the importance of communication routes into the highlands. Although the mound-circle architectural elements tie Pallka firmly with long-standing coastal traditions, the physical arrangement, especially the subsidiary lateral position of the circle, suggests a different set of values or priorities which may be attributable to the great distance from the coast, conflicting local influences, or both. Much of the ceramic inventory of Pallka documents its occupation well into the Early Horizon, but a portion of the collection establishes ties to the coast, especially Las Haldas, and is critical in defining the Initial Period component of the site. Ceramic connections between Pallka and Las Haldas, and by extension between Pallka and the Sechin Alto Complex, are surprising because Pallka and Pampa de las Llamas-Moxeke both occupy the Casma branch of the river. This suggests that the polity centered within the Sechin Alto Complex was the stronger of the two coexisting polities.

In terms of sheer magnitude of construction projects, the high point of Casma Valley development occurred during the Initial Period. At this time, the Sechin Alto Complex was at its apogee, and Pampa de las Llamas-Moxeke was a major settlement in its own right. Sechin Alto was certainly the largest mound structure in the New World at that time. Furthermore, the complex which Sechin Alto dominated, with an area of at least 10.5 square kilometers, was larger than many subsequent polity capitals. The pattern of large inland sites associated with subsidiary coastal communities is also clear. The Las Haldas temple, truly one of the most spectacular Initial Period coastal sites, is nevertheless "subsidiary" in comparison to Sechin Alto, and Tortugas had a comparable relationship to Pampa de las Llamas-Moxeke.

Survey data from sites farther inland suggest that the polity centered in the Sechin branch had the greater influence. It appears that long-distance trade with the highlands may have become increasingly important to the major inland centers near the coast, which initially had a primarily agricultural focus.

Significantly, most of the major Casma Valley Initial Period sites yielded clear evidence that their development had ended abruptly. The final temple at Las Haldas appears to have been under construction (Grieder 1975: 103), and it lacks the associated refuse and ceramics indicative of a substantial occupation. Sechin Bajo and Taukachi-Konkan are so barren of early midden that their chronological placement was hampered, and major mounds at both locations are clearly unfinished. Although Pampa de las Llamas-Moxeke has ample evidence of an extended period of occupation, there is evidence that many of the intermediate-sized mounds were under construction but never completed. These data strongly point to an episode of severe disruption near the end of the Initial Period.

Early Horizon

Julio C. Tello devoted a substantial portion of his life to defining and promoting the existence of a third "horizon" or pan-Andean phenomenon which predated the previously recognized Inca and Tiahuanaco/Huari horizons (Tello 1943). This "Early Horizon" was characterized by widespread manifestations of the Chavin phenomenon, which has been variously called a religious cult, an art style, and a culture (Bennett and Bird 1964: 93; Bushnell 1965: 43; Lanning 1967: 98; Lumbreras 1974: 57; Mason 1969: 43; Willey 1971: 116). Especially pertinent here is the widely held idea that the earliest Andean civilization was the product of Chavin and its widespread influence. While the Initial Period was seen as essentially a time of maintaining status quo, innovations such as monumental architecture, irrigation agriculture, and a truly great art style were attributed to the Chavin culture. Before radiocarbon dating was widely used, the extent of Chavin influence was defined on the basis of stylistic comparisons of early iconography. This led, for example, to the inclusion of Moxeke, Cerro Blanco, and Punkurí within the Chavin region of influence. Largely on the basis of recently available radiocarbon dates for coastal sites as well as for Chavin de Huantar, it has become increasingly apparent that most major coastal developments occurred during the Initial Period (Burger 1978: 358–389, 1981: 596–600; T. Pozorski 1983; T. Pozorski and S. Pozorski, in press b). The Casma Valley data go a long way toward documenting the truly spectacular Initial Period developments while also filling the newly created Early Horizon "void" by providing data on events within the valley during the later period.

The Casma Valley occupation which appears at the end of the Initial Period and spans the Early Horizon differs so markedly from earlier Initial Period sites that we consider outside invasion a likely explanation for the changes. These differences permeate the architectural, artifact, and subsistence data from securely dated Early Horizon sites, and additional evidence supports this interpretation. The unfinished aspects of many earlier Initial Period sites suggest that their development was abruptly halted and the sites suddenly abandoned—a scenario readily attributable to a hostile invasion. We also feel that the Cerro Sechin stone carvings depict the victory of the invaders over the local population.

Excavation data for the Early Horizon in the Casma Valley come from the single component sites of Pampa Rosario and San Diego as well as the posttemple component of Las Haldas. Radiocarbon dates indicate that the three sites are not entirely contemporaneous, though there is considerable overlap. The posttemple Las Haldas occupation appears to be the earliest, followed soon after by Pampa Rosario, which was occupied for a substantial time before the establishment of San Diego.

The two large settlements of Pampa Rosario and San Diego are very similar. They share a new architectural form characterized by repetitive courts and small platforms with paired ramps, but *no large mounds*. Court and platform units are scattered across the site; there is no longer a central site axis. The ceramic inventories of Pampa Rosario and San Diego are dominated by panpipes, flaring-rim jars, thick stirrup spouts, a rare ceramic club head, and the use of circles and dots, exterior net or fabric impressions, and white paint—all vessel shapes and surface treatments without known local antecedents. Ground stone blades are also present at both sites. In contrast, the Las Haldas Early Horizon architecture was clearly ephemeral, and the associated midden yielded virtually no artifacts.

The establishment of posttemple Las Haldas, Pampa Rosario, and San Diego was accompanied by the introduction of maize to the Casma Valley—not gradually but immediately, in quantities that dominated the floral inventory. One maize cache at San Diego yielded fifty-one whole cobs with kernels as well as accompanying complete stalks. The popularity of maize at this early date may well be attributable to its value for brewing *chicha*, or maize beer, and large neckless ollas documented for Pampa Rosario and San Diego may have been used in the brewing process. Possibly as significant as the rapid acceptance of maize is the near absence of *lúcuma* at all excavated Early Horizon sites. *Lúcuma* fruit had been an important food in Casma since preceramic times, and its remains are well represented in the Initial Period middens of Pampa de las Llamas-Moxeke, Tortugas, and Las Haldas.

The relative size of San Diego and Pampa Rosario and their respective coastal and inland locations immediately suggest the possibility of a traditional coastal-inland exchange system linking the two sites. This was clearly *not* the case during the Early Horizon. Pampa Rosario was definitely an agriculturally oriented site, and the nature of the plant remains from San Diego indicates that this site's inhabitants were also doing their own farming. Cotton boll fragments and bean pods are common at both sites, and the presence of whole maize stalks at San Diego provides clear evidence of direct access to cultivated fields. Unlike Tortugas or Las Haldas, San Diego is located near arable land, and the nature of the plant remains from this Early Horizon site indicates that agriculture was the main focus. The relatively late Early Horizon date of San Diego and the site's location considerably downvalley from Pampa Rosario suggest that the site may have been established to open additional lower-valley zones to cultivation.

Complementing the agricultural focus at Pampa Rosario and San Diego is a new emphasis on domesticated land mammals as a source of animal protein. Marine shellfish and fish continued to provide a substantial part of the animal-protein intake, especially at San Diego, but the introduction of domesticated camelids and guinea pigs provided an important new reliable protein source. These domesticates also appeared suddenly in the Casma Valley along with the new architecture, artifacts, and maize.

The posttemple occupation of Las Haldas is also largely contemporary with the Early Horizon agricultural sites, especially Pampa Rosario. The associated midden has a very different character compared to both contemporary inland and earlier coastal examples because chiton plates and remains of sea urchins as well as stalks from marine algae predominate. It may be significant that chitons and sea urchins are among the more visible and accessible of the large shellfish species. They could have been easily taken even by persons unaccustomed to marine resource exploitation. Both the associated architecture and the rarity of artifacts reflect the temporary nature of the occupation. This architecture consists only of low wind screens built from cobbles and boulders pulled from the temple facings. These structures sit atop the Initial Period temple, nestled in areas protected from the wind. Based on these data, the posttemple Las Haldas occupation appears very different from earlier coastal settlements because the species inventory is so restricted and the associated occupation so ephemeral.

Thus, excavation data from Pampa Rosario, San Diego, and posttemple Las Haldas reveal that virtually every aspect of the Casma Valley life-style had changed drastically. The change in architecture, the appearance of totally new ceramic forms and decorative techniques, and a revamped subsistence inventory which emphasized agricultural products, especially maize, and introduced an alternative to marine resources in the form of domesticated mammals all happened suddenly. We feel these discontinuities with earlier developments are best explained by an invasion from the outside which occurred near the end of the Initial Period.

We have assigned additional surveyed sites to the Early Horizon largely on the basis of ceramics and architecture. Features of these sites serve to flesh out the invasion scenario and also document subsequent developments within the Casma Valley during the Early Horizon.

Ceramic and radiocarbon evidence from Cerro Sechin indicate that, in addition to its early Initial Period component, it was also occupied during the Initial Period/Early Horizon transition and through at least part of the Early Horizon. Of special interest to us is the outer temple adorned by stone carvings. Based on the recently published associated radiocarbon date of 1290 ± 20 B.C. and thermoluminescent date of 1290 ± 240 B.C. (Samaniego et al. 1985: 182–184), we would tentatively place this carved stone facade in the early part of this time span. The carvings on this facade have long been interpreted as commemorating a battle, with the victors graphically slaughtering the conquered (Bueno and Samaniego 1969: Samaniego 1973). The victors are clearly warriors, and their dress for battle differs markedly from the costume of the defeated. These unfortunates wear a pleated skirt or kilt with a scalloped tunic which closely resembles the clothing of the frieze figures of Moxeke, a comparison which Roe (1974: 34) made for the purpose of chronological assessments. Taking this comparison a step further, we feel that the indigenous inhabitants of the lower valley were the victims in this massacre recorded in stone. Furthermore, since the monumental iconography of Moxeke probably depicts very important beings—rulers, priests, or deities—it appears likely that the skirt/tunic costume was the clothing of the local elite who governed the population. Following this reasoning, it appears likely that the Cerro Sechin stone carvings commemorate the gory deposition of indigenous leaders by the invading group.

The success of the invaders over what clearly had been powerful and rapidly developing polities may have been due to their military tactics. There is no artifactual evidence that the indigenous polities were warlike. However, the Early Horizon artifact inventory included a club head, and the conquering figures on the stone carvings are clearly outfitted for war. Equally significant is the vicious manner in which the victims were mutilated and dismembered, because such tactics would have been especially devastating to a nonmilitant population. Finally, the early radiocarbon dates associated with the carvings chronologically place the time of the invasion as late in the Initial Period. This generally coincides with terminal dates for the Initial Period sites and is earlier than the dates for excavated Early Horizon sites. The later Early Horizon dates for Pampa Rosario and especially San Diego may reflect the fact that such major settlements were established gradually as the area was settled.

On the basis of artifactual evidence, we believe the sites of Pallka and Huaca Desvio have Early Horizon components. We have already presented arguments for the establishment of Pallka during the Initial Period, and there is no obvious surface evidence of local rebuilding before the much later adobe structures. The artifact assemblage there also contains examples of ground stone blades, panpipes, flaring rims, and thick stirrup spouts, as well as the use of circles and dots and exterior fabric impression—all elements defined at Pampa Rosario and San Diego. However, the Initial Period and Early Horizon ceramics known from the lower Casma Valley do not overlap completely with the range of ceramics documented for Pallka. This remaining portion of the assemblage, which Tello (1956: 36–48) illustrated well, documents interaction between Pallka and zones above the Casma Valley, including Chavin de Huantar (Burger 1978: 36–48; Tello 1960: 325–348). Polished slate blades have also been found at Chavin de Huantar. Although Tello attributed these to the later Early Intermediate Period Huaylas culture (Tello 1960: 308–312), they may be earlier and reflect late Early Horizon interaction with the coast. The varied artifact inventory of Pallka is in keeping with its location at an intersection of major communication routes between the coast and highlands.

We assign Huaca Desvio to the Early Horizon mainly on the basis of ceramic evidence. The form and very existence of the three mounds which comprise the site as well as the presence of an approximately circular court argue for connections with the earlier Initial Period coastal tradition. However, since no clearly earlier ceramics were recovered during survey, it appears that the configuration of Huaca Desvio may be attributed to both the spatial and chronological distance between it and the lower-valley sites. Sherds from Huaca Desvio do exhibit traits which tie the site to Pampa Rosario and San Diego downvalley. Several of these elements, especially the circle-and-dot motif, occur in unusually high frequencies at Huaca Desvio compared to the lower-valley sites. Significantly, the same set of associated ceramic traits, plus ground slate blades, are very common at sites in the upper Nepeña drainage immediately to the north (R. Daggett 1984: 182–190). The increasing frequency of certain of these diagnostic elements as one moves spatially from Pampa Rosario and San Diego to Huaca Desvio and finally the upper Nepeña Valley argues for their source in that highland vicinity or even farther north and east.

Probably slightly later in the Early Horizon, the sites of Chankillo and La Cantina were established on the Casma branch of the river. We base this later chronological placement mainly on evidence from surface ceramic collections, architectural traits, and radiocarbon dates. Both sites share common ceramic traits which connect them chronologically with the Early Horizon sites of Pampa Rosario and San Diego, but other elements of the ceramic inventories serve to extend the duration of their occupation slightly longer. Huaca Desvio and Pallka also yielded later ceramics and therefore probably also continued to be occupied during this time.

La Cantina is unusual because it is one of only two sites of this time period which are dominated by a mound structure. The other example is Huaca Desvio. The orientation of La Cantina is coincident with that of Pampa de las Llamas-Moxeke—a feature which might indicate either a very early date, despite the absence of early sherds, or an anachronistic adherence to old patterns—the interpretation we favor. In addition to the central mound, the site contains several plazas extending toward the northeast; one of these is now badly damaged. The arrangement of these plazas and the access by way of inset stairs is very similar to examples from the west plain of Chankillo, thereby arguing for the contemporaneity of the two sites.

The radiocarbon dates of 342 ± 80 B.C. and 120 ± 100 B.C. from Chankillo help locate these two sites within the chronological framework. Both architecture and midden associated with settlements in the vicinity of Chankillo cover a large area and document the local existence of a substantial population. Like Pampa Rosario and San Diego, much of the Chankillo occupation is domestic, but the two labyrinthine compounds and especially the Thirteen Steps probably had a nondomestic, and potentially a ceremonial, function.

The fortress of Chankillo is especially significant, however, because it is among the earliest evidence of fortification within the Casma Valley. The fortress on top of the hill of Cerro Sechin which was surveyed by

Thompson (1964a: 210, 1974: 16, fig. 5) has also been dated to this time period. The construction of these two fortresses may be taken as further evidence of the existence of a more warlike population in the lower valley. It is interesting that the first fortifications in valleys farther north also appear at this time (Topic and Topic, in press; Willey 1953: 358–359; Wilson 1983, in press). This suggests that an increased potential for warfare and a concomitant need for protection was becoming widespread near the end of the Early Horizon and the beginning of the succeeding Early Intermediate Period.

Data from the Casma Valley indicate that the Early Horizon was marked by an initial phase of disruption because of invasion followed by a period of local settling in and adjustment. The Cerro Sechin carvings provide graphic evidence of the nature of the conquest, and the associated radiocarbon dates reveal that it occurred quite early.

The Las Haldas posttemple occupation is also significant because it reflects the attitude of the Early Horizon Casma Valley residents toward the temples of earlier people. By robbing stones from the temple facing for use in their temporary structures, by building these windscreens in the heart of the temple for protection from the wind, and by indiscriminately dumping garbage over major elements of the earlier architecture (e.g., the central staircase), the posttemple occupants showed a clear disregard, and perhaps disdain, for the former importance and sacred aspect of the Las Haldas temple. Ceramic evidence from the Moxeke mound, Sechin Alto, and Cerro Sechin suggests that these predominantly Initial Period sites were also at least briefly occupied by the conquerors of Casma. Such reoccupation of the loci of power of the early polities demonstrated both a supremacy over the indigenous group and deliberate disregard for the sacred nature of their temples. Such an attitude would be expected from members of an invading group. This immediate desecration of Initial Period power centers probably represents the initial thrust of the invaders into the valleys. It was followed by the establishment of the more substantial and permanent settlements of Pampa Rosario and San Diego which typified the lifeways of the intrusive population.

The intrusive population was accomplished at both agriculture and animal husbandry. Gradually these people moved into the valley, establishing substantial settlements built according to their own architectural tenets. They were less interested in traditional marine resources than the indigenous population had been, since they brought domesticated animals, and they introduced and emphasized maize as an agricultural staple. The appearance of fortifications within Casma and along much of the north suggests that warfare or the threat of warfare was becoming increasingly common.

SUMMARY AND CONCLUSIONS

Recent investigations of the Casma Valley have yielded important data to document several new developments during the early prehistory of the area. The time span from the Cotton Preceramic through the end of the Early Horizon (2500–200 B.C.) was successively characterized by:

1. The establishment of large prepottery coastal settlements with a fairly complex social organization—a phenomenon common to much of the north and central Andean coast.

2. Spectacular developments during the Initial Period which are largely attributable to the technological innovation of irrigation agriculture. During this time span, at least one of the polities centered in Casma was among the most advanced in the New World.

3. The abrupt truncation of Initial Period development by invaders from outside the Casma Valley near the end of the Initial Period.

4. Settlement and exploitation of the Casma Valley by the new arrivals, who introduced a markedly different life-style that was followed through the end of the Early Horizon.

During this critical early time span, there is considerable variation in the degree to which events in the Casma Valley parallel developments in other areas. We explore the applicability of Casma Valley data to other parts of the Andes more fully in this section.

During the late Cotton Preceramic Period, substantial preceramic occupations were present at Huaynuná and Las Haldas, respectively, to the north and south of the Casma Valley. The people at each site were essentially self-sufficient, living off marine resources supplemented by products they cultivated on floodplain plots in the Casma Valley. In view of the mound structures at Huaynuná, it is possible that at least the more northern settlement had an incipient chiefdom level of social organization, though more definite evidence for this supposition is lacking. The people living at these sites, possibly in conjunction with people living at the preceramic sites of Culebras in the Culebras Valley to the south and Los Chinos in the Nepeña Valley to the north, formed the population base for subsequent developments in the Casma Valley.

Huaynuná and preceramic Las Haldas are typical of late Cotton Preceramic developments which occurred all along the north and central

Andean coast. These sites are all very similar, sharing a marine-resource focus and an emphasis on industrial cultigens. Most of the larger examples contain architecture, including substantial mounds. Moseley (1975) has argued that the abundance and perennial availability of marine resources allowed the establishment of sizable permanent settlements and thereby preadapted the populations to conditions of increasing social complexity. Also significant is the probable existence of an intersite communication network at this time (T. Pozorski and S. Pozorski, in press b), something suggested by the high coincidence of artifact inventories among sites—largely in terms of the technology best suited for marine exploitation, but also in terms of aspects such as twined textile manufacture. This preexisting communication system was a key factor in the rapid spread of technological innovations during the succeeding period.

During the Initial Period, irrigation technology as well as pottery and weaving were introduced to the Casma Valley. The potential of irrigation agriculture was quickly realized, and it soon resulted in the inland establishment of such large sites as Pampa de las Llamas-Moxeke and Sechin Alto by at least 1500 B.C. Because of the continued need for animal protein which was traditionally marine in origin, ties with the seacoast were not entirely broken. Exchange systems were established between Pampa de las Llamas-Moxeke and its coastal colony of Tortugas and between the inland Sechin Alto Complex and Las Haldas on the coast. Both inland sites provided agricultural products in exchange for shellfish and fish collected at the coastal settlements.

During the Initial Period in the Casma Valley, monumental mound construction reached its apogee, never to be equalled during subsequent prehistoric or historic periods. Pampa de las Llamas-Moxeke covered over 2 square kilometers and at least one mound, Moxeke, was decorated with enormous polychrome adobe friezes. The inner adobe temple construction of Cerro Sechin as well as Sechin Alto was completed quite early and decorated with friezes and murals. The additional construction of Sechin Bajo and Taukachi-Konkan made the resultant Sechin Alto Complex, which covered at least 10.5 square kilometers, the largest mound site in the New World at that time. These polities also influenced sites much farther inland, and Pallka may have been established at a key crossroad to control or take advantage of trade within the upper reaches of the valley. Clearly the Initial Period polities were very advanced and had attained a state level of political development.

It is significant that no maize was present during the Initial Period in the Casma Valley. This evidence supports the view that substantial social development can occur with a subsistence base of a wide variety of agricultural foods in conjunction with marine resources, but without maize.

In general, the Casma Valley is typical of Initial Period developments along much of the Peruvian coast. It has become increasingly clear that the Initial Period was a time of especially rapid and spectacular early development—far more so than the succeeding Early Horizon. At this time there was a proliferation of substantial mound-dominated sites at inland locations especially propitious for canal irrigation. In at least one additional valley, Moche, close ties between inland and coastal sites have been demonstrated (S. Pozorski and T. Pozorski 1979a). The "innovation" of irrigation agriculture spread so rapidly along existing communication networks that its adoption—reflected by the rise of substantial inland sites—appears instantaneous in the archaeological record. Some valleys such as Moche to the north (T. Pozorski 1976) and Supe to the south (Feldman 1980: 211; Kosok 1965: 217–226) contain unusually large concentrations of inland mound sites. Like Casma, where mound sites are also concentrated, each of these valleys may have formed the nucleus of a more far-reaching polity which loosely united several coastal valleys (T. Pozorski and S. Pozorski, in press b). However, despite the abundance of mound sites in certain valleys, no single mound is comparable in size to Sechin Alto, and the Sechin Alto Complex is unequalled in size and complexity. Thus the Casma Valley is also unique for the Initial Period because its sites are the largest and its polities the most complex examples known for that time.

Catastrophe visited the Casma Valley at the end of the Initial Period, and a new way of life characterized the subsequent Early Horizon. Outside invaders, probably from the upper Nepeña Valley or a source farther north and east, conquered the mighty Casma Valley polities. Of the coastal valleys, Casma contained substantial polities, one of which was the largest known, with influence extending into the upper reaches of the valley. This locus of power concentration on the coast may well have been what specifically attracted the invaders to Casma. The shock of facing militant invaders undoubtedly contributed to the downfall of the Casma groups, who apparently had no history of warfare. It is also evident, however, that the invading group was an especially gruesome lot who decapitated and mutilated their victims in the manner so vividly depicted on the Cerro Sechin stone carvings. They also briefly occupied major sites, including the Moxeke mound, Cerro Sechin, Sechin Alto, and Las Haldas. This served to reinforce the authority of the new group while also violating and desecrating the very structures which had previously symbolized the power of the Initial Period polities.

The invading group brought in maize and domesticated animals, along with distinct pottery and artifacts. New sites such as Huaca Desvio, Pampa Rosario, and San Diego were established, but there is little evidence of centralized authority because these sites lack the large and precisely laid out mounds and plazas of the earlier Initial Period sites. Instead, the new architecture seems distinctly more secular. It seems likely that Casma was administered from the highlands during the Early Horizon, and this may be a major reason that the site of Pallka apparently flourished—its elaborate pottery reflects interaction with both the coast and highlands. Sites continued to be established within the Casma Valley, one of the most noteworthy being the occupation of the Chankillo area. Compounds, smaller structures, and extensive midden there attest to a sizable settlement, whereas the enigmatic Thirteen Steps seem to represent the only known truly ceremonial coastal architecture attributable to the intrusive polity. Finally, the hilltop fortress indicates a growing need to establish defensible positions.

What can we really say about the invaders who conquered the lower Casma Valley? Where were they from and how much did their invasion of Casma affect other areas during the Early Horizon? Assuming an Initial Period date for most of the developments once attributed to the Chavin phenomenon, *what was happening* to fill this newly created Early Horizon void?

The invading group appears most likely to have come from the highlands, probably to the north and east of the Casma Valley. This area of origin is hypothesized on the basis of specific ceramic traits and artifacts known from Pampa Rosario, San Diego, and Huaca Desvio, which seem to intensify as one moves from southwest to northeast toward the middle and upper reaches of the Nepeña Valley (R. Daggett 1984; Proulx 1985).

The surveys that Richard Daggett (1984) and Donald Proulx (1985) conducted revealed dozens of Early Horizon sites in Nepeña. However, neither investigator conducted any excavations or obtained any absolute dates, so their interpretations are limited to arguments based on similiary seriation and comparisons to material from other areas of Peru. Proulx (1985: 189) states that the prominent circle-and-dot ceramic motif characterizes the first two-thirds of the Early Horizon, which, according to his dating, spans 1300 to 700 B.C. This assertion seems invalid, however, in light of assemblages containing the motif from the Late Capilla Phase at Huaricoto (Burger 1985: 519–527) and the Janabarriu Phase at Chavin de Huantar (Burger 1979, 1981: 595, 1985: 507) that date between 400 and 200 B.C. By contrast, Daggett (1984: 439) correlates the circle-and-dot motif (from his Early Horizon Phase I) with the Janabarriu Phase at Chavin de Huantar.

Indeed, many elements of Daggett's Early Horizon Phases I and II assemblages are present in the Early Horizon assemblages in the Casma Valley, particularly at Pampa Rosario, San Diego, and Huaca Desvio. These elements include ceramic decoration using circles and dots (R. Daggett 1984: 134, figs. 5-1, 5-4), zoned white paint (R. Daggett 1984: fig. 5-6), and exterior fabric impressions (R. Daggett 1984: fig. 6-8) as well as the presence of ceramic panpipes (R. Daggett 1984: 135, 258), flaring-rim jars (R. Daggett 1984: fig. 6-5), and ground stone blades (R. Daggett 1984: 135, 258, fig. 5-23). Despite the similarities between the Nepeña and Casma assemblages, the Nepeña Valley does not appear to be the ultimate source of these traits and the culture that was associated with them. Daggett (1984: 231, 254, in press) sees highland settlers moving into the upper reaches of the Nepeña Valley, whereas Proulx (1985: 257– 258) sees strong cultural influence emanating from the highlands, ultimately from Chavin de Huantar.

A possible general area of origin for the proposed invaders is the Callejon de Huaylas, a suggestion supported by the presence of Cerro Sechin– like carvings there (Thompson 1962b). However, it is not likely to be near the site of Huaricoto, where the Late Capilla Phase, containing decorative elements (circles and dots; Burger 1985: figs. 40, 41c, 50a, 50b, 50d) and forms (thick, flanged stirrup spouts and panpipes; Burger 1985: figs. 36–38, 49) similar to those of the Early Horizon Casma Valley assemblages dates later—between 400 and 200 B.C. (Burger 1985: 507, 519). The architectural forms at Huaricoto are also distinct from contemporary Casma Valley examples (Burger and Salazar-Burger 1980, 1985). It is also possible that the area of origin is somewhat north of the Callejon de Huaylas. At the site of Huacaloma, near Cajamarca, the Late Huacaloma Period, dated to 820 ± 80 B.C., contains distinctive zoned-white painted pottery with incisions (Huacaloma White-on-Red; Terada and Onuki 1982: 253, pl. 29b, c) virtually identical to that at San Diego and Pampa Rosario. The same phase also contains ground stone blades (Terada and Onuki 1982: 203, pl. 54, nos. 1–4, 8). The associated date at Huacaloma is earlier than dates at Huaricoto, but it must be pointed out that the zoned-white painted pottery and ground stone blades are only two of several elements that make up the intrusive Early Horizon

Casma Valley assemblages and are only minor elements in the overall assemblage at Huacaloma proper.

It seems more likely that the area of origin for the highland invaders of the lower Casma Valley lies somewhere between Cajamarca and the Callejon de Huaylas. The invaders probably entered the upper Nepeña Valley and especially the upper Casma Valley (Sechin branch) near the end of the Initial Period. The diffusion of the influence of this culture and associated cultural elements was felt somewhat later in such Early Horizon sites as Huaricoto and Chavin de Huantar.

The impact of the invasion in Casma is clearly manifested in truncated Initial Period development, intrusive architecture and artifacts, and the commemorative panels of Cerro Sechin. However, there is no conclusive evidence that other coastal valleys were physically conquered in the same manner. The invaders were apparently attracted to Casma as the seat of the most advanced polities, but once Casma fell, nearby valleys offered no resistance. These same valleys, Nepeña and Huarmey, had probably been influenced, if not controlled, from Casma during the Initial period. Subsequent Early Horizon artifacts and settlements in these areas (R. Daggett, in press; Kosok 1965: 208–209, figs. 20, 21; Proulx 1968: 71–72; Thompson 1966) indicate that they also came under the intrusive highland polity that defeated Casma. The result was a political unit extending from the north-central highlands to the north-central coast, but apparently centered in the sierra. This development was unprecedented in Andean prehistory and was not duplicated until several centuries later, during the Tiahuanaco/Huari expansion.

Data from valleys farther north reveal a defensive response to developments to the south as well as possibly some degree of influence from the emerging highland/coastal polity. Survey data from the Santa (Wilson 1983, in press) and Viru valleys (Willey 1953) document a clustering of Early Horizon and subsequent early Early Intermediate Period settlements in the upper reaches of both valleys, as well as the first appearance of fortifications—most of which are on the *south* sides of both valleys. This appears to be a direct response to danger or unrest originating in the south and east—the source area postulated for the conquerors of Casma—but there is no evidence that the valleys north of Nepeña were ever directly controlled from the highlands. Rather, the local polity centered in Moche was probably maintained. However, elements of the artifact inventory of the invaders apparently did diffuse north, including traits such as circle-and-dot ceramic decoration and slate blades (Brennan 1978: 669–672; Mujica 1975: 312–325; T. Pozorski 1976).

As was the case for the Initial Period, certain developments within the Casma Valley are unique for the Early Horizon. Most notable is the invasion of the valley and the resultant establishment of the highland/coastal polity. This polity encompassed a substantial portion of the north-central coast, making its study important to the definition of the Early Horizon as a whole. Excavation data from the Casma Valley sites of Pampa Rosario and San Diego take on added importance because the highland portion of this political unit is so poorly known. Despite the intrusive group's ability to defeat Casma, its influence was not so widespread as to suggest a true horizon style, and local developments continued well to the north and presumably also on the central coast. Thus, the Early Horizon appears to have been a period of fragmentation characterized by numerous local developments, including the highland/coastal polity of the Casma area.

In conclusion, we feel that we have made significant progress toward the accomplishment of the major objectives of the Casma Valley study. First, we have been very successful in placing the excavated sites within a chronological framework. Radiocarbon dates were critical to meeting this goal, especially as we assessed Initial Period sites. Precise absolute dating allowed us to appreciate the magnitude of Initial Period development and to recognize the simultaneous existence of two major polities within the valley. By building on this relatively precise chronology for the six excavated sites, we were able tentatively to assign relative chronological positions to surveyed sites.

We located midden deposits rich in plant and animal remains at each of the tested sites, so our efforts to study subsistence changes through time were also highly successful. Some of these results were both startling and highly significant. Preceramic Huaynuná yielded a variety of cultigens, but the tubers recovered were especially significant because such a variety and quantity had not previously been documented. The Initial Period subsistence inventory was important not only because of the *addition* of peanuts but also because of the *absence* of maize. This is particularly significant in light of the magnitude of Initial Period monumental constructions. Finally, subsistence data were a major factor in identifying the drastic changes which occurred at the end of the Initial Period as an invasion. The new residents brought with them domesticated animals and maize, which they clearly preferred to some of the traditional foods such as *lúcuma*.

As we predicted, successful accomplishment of the first two objectives was critical to a realization of the third goal: understanding the processual development of early Casma Valley society. Successfully ordering a majority of the sites chronologically and documenting major subsistence shifts has brought us closer to an understanding of the processual development. Additional data, especially from the excavated sites and Cerro Sechin, were also critical. Using all these sources it has been possible to begin to reconstruct the *process* of developments in the Casma Valley. We have identified an Initial Period florescence and the subsequent external invasion which successfully crushed indigenous opposition and implemented a new life-style. Yet addressing this objective has raised as many questions as it has answered. These new questions are crucial ones involving such topics as the nature of state-level polity development during the Initial Period and the source area and motivation of the population which conquered Casma. The generation of such new avenues of inquiry is a vital part of the successful realization of the project goals.

References Cited

ALARCO, EUGENIO
1975   *Las Piedras Grabadas de Sechin.* Editorial Ausonia–Talleres Gráficos, Lima.

ALVA, WALTER
1978   "Las Salinas de Chao: Un Complejo Precerámico." In *El Hombre y la Cultura Andina*, vol. 1, edited by Ramiro Matos, pp. 275–276. III Congreso Peruano, Actas y Trabajos, Lima.

BENNETT, WENDELL C., AND JUNIUS B. BIRD
1964   *Andean Culture History.* The Natural History Museum Press, Garden City, New York:

BERGER, R., G. J. FERGUSON, AND W. F. LIBBY
1965   "UCLA Radiocarbon Dates IV." *Radiocarbon* 7: 347.

BONAVIA, DUCCIO
1974   *Ricchata Quellccani: Murallas Pintadas Prehispánicas.* Fondo del Libro del Banco Industrial del Perú, Lima.

BRENNAN, CURTISS
1978   "Investigations at Cerro Arena, Peru: Incipient Urbanism of the Peruvian North Coast." Ph.D. dissertation, University of Arizona, Tucson. University Microfilms, Ann Arbor.

BUENO, ALBERTO, AND LORENZO SAMANIEGO
1969   "Hallazgos Recientes en Sechin." *Amaru* 11: 31–38.

BURGER, RICHARD L.
1978   "The Occupation of Chavin, Ancash, in the Initial Period and Early Horizon." Ph.D. dissertation, University of California, Berkeley. University Microfilms, Ann Arbor.
1979   "Resultados Preliminarios de Excavaciones en los Distritos de Chavín de Huantar y San Marcos, Perú." In *Arqueología Peruana: Investigaciones Arqueológicas en el Perú, 1976 Seminario*, edited by Ramiro Matos, pp. 133–155. Intercambio Educativo entre los Estados Unidos y el Perú, Lima.
1981   "The Radiocarbon Evidence for the Temporal Priority of Chavin de Huantar." *American Antiquity* 46: 592–602.
1985   "Prehistoric Stylistic Change and Cultural Development at Huaricoto, Peru." *National Geographic Research* 1 (4): 505–534.

BURGER, RICHARD L., AND LUCY SALAZAR-BURGER
  1980   "Ritual and Religion at Huaricoto." *Archaeology* 33 (6): 26–32.
  1985   "The Early Ceremonial Center of Huaricoto." In *Early Ceremonial Architecture in the Andes*, edited by Christopher B. Donnan, pp. 111–135. Dumbarton Oaks, Washington, D.C.
BUSHNELL, G. W. S.
  1963   *Peru*. Thames and Hudson, London.
CARDENAS, MERCEDES
  1979   *A Chronology of the Use of Marine Resources in Ancient Peru*. Pontífica Universidad Católica del Perú, Lima.
CARLEVATO, DENISE C.
  1979   "Analysis of Ceramics from the Casma Valley, Peru: Implications for the Local Chronology." Master's thesis, Department of Anthropology, University of Wisconsin, Madison.
CIEZA DE LEÓN, PEDRO
  1973   *La Crónica del Perú*. Originally published 1553. Ediciones Peisa, Lima.
COLLIER, DONALD
  1962   Archaeological Investigations in the Casma Valley, Peru. *Thirty-fourth International Congress of Americanists:* 411–417. Vienna.
CONKLIN, WILLIAM J.
  1974   "Pampa Gramalote Textiles." In *Irene Emery Roundtable on Museum Textiles, 1974 Proceedings: Archaeological Textiles*, edited by Patricia L. Fiske, pp. 77–92. The Textile Museum, Washington, D.C.
CRAIG, ALAN K., AND NORBERT P. PSUTY
  1968   *The Paracas Papers: Studies in Marine Desert Ecology*. Occasional Publications 1. Department of Geography, Florida Atlantic University.
DAGGETT, CHERYL
  1983   "Casma Incised Pottery: An Analysis of Collections from the Nepeña Valley." In *Investigations of the Andean Past*, edited by Daniel H. Sandweiss, pp. 209–225. Papers from the First Annual Northeast Conference on Andean Archaeology and Ethnohistory, Cornell University, Ithaca.
DAGGETT, RICHARD
  1984   "The Early Horizon Occupation of the Nepeña Valley, North Central Coast of Peru." Ph.D. dissertation, University of Massachusetts, Amherst. University Microfilms, Ann Arbor.
  in   "Toward the Development of the State on the North Central Coast
  press   of Peru." In *The Origins and Development of the Andean State*, edited by Jonathan Haas, Shelia Pozorski, and Thomas Pozorski. Cambridge University Press, Cambridge.
ENGEL, FREDERIC
  1957a "Early Sites on the Peruvian Coast." *Southwestern Journal of Anthropology* 13: 54–68.
  1957b "Sites et Établissements sans Céramique de la Côte Peruvienne." *Journal de la Société des Americanistes*, New Series 46: 67–155.
  1963   "A Preceramic Settlement on the Central Coast of Peru: Asia, Unit 1."

American Philosophical Society Transactions, New Series 53 (3): 1–139.

1966   *Geografía Humana Prehistórica y Agricultura Precolombina de la Quebrada de Chilca, I*. Oficina de Promoción y Desarrollo, Departamento de Publicaciones, Universidad Agraria, Lima.

1967   "Le Complexe Précéramique d'El Paraiso (Perou)." *Journal de la Société des Americanistes*, New Series 55: 43–95.

1970   *Las Lomas de Iguanil y el Complejo de Haldas*. Departamento de Publicaciones, Universidad Agraria, Lima.

FELDMAN, ROBERT A.
1980   "Aspero, Peru: Architecture, Subsistence Economy, and Other Artifacts of a Preceramic Maritime Chiefdom." Ph.D. dissertation, Department of Anthropology, Harvard University, Cambridge.

1985   "Preceramic Corporate Architecture: Evidence for the Development of Non-Egalitarian Social Systems in Peru." In *Early Ceremonial Architecture in the Andes*, edited by Christopher B. Donnan, pp. 71–92. Dumbarton Oaks, Washington, D.C.

FUNG, ROSA
1969   "Las Aldas: Su Ubicación dentro del Proceso Histórico del Perú Antiguo." *Dédalo* 5 (9–10): 1–208.

1972   "Nuevos Datos para el Periódo de Cerámica Inicial en el Valle de Casma." *Arqueología y Sociedad* 7–8: 1–12.

FUNG, ROSA, AND VÍCTOR PIMENTEL
1973   "Chankillo." *Revista del Museo Nacional* 39: 71–80.

FUNG, ROSA, AND CARLOS WILLIAMS
1977   "Exploraciones y Excavaciones en el Valle de Sechín, Casma." *Revista del Museo Nacional* 43: 111–155.

GRIEDER, TERENCE
1975   "A Dated Sequence of Building and Pottery at Las Haldas." *Ñawpa Pacha* 13: 99–112.

ISHIDA, EIICHIRO, ET AL.
1960   *Andes 1: University of Tokyo Scientific Expedition to the Andes in 1958*. Bijutsushuppansha, Tokyo.

IZUMI, SEIICHI, AND KAZUO TERADA
1972   *Excavations at Kotosh, Peru: A Report on the Third and Fourth Expeditions*. University of Tokyo Press, Tokyo.

JIMENEZ BORJA, ARTURO
1969   "El Estilo Sechín." *Amaru* 11: 39–41.

KAUFFMANN, FEDERICO
1980   *Manual de Arqueología Peruana*. Iberia, Lima.

KOSOK, PAUL
1965   *Life, Land and Water in Ancient Peru*. Long Island University Press, New York.

KROEBER, ALFRED
1944   *Peruvian Archaeology in 1942*. Viking Fund Publication in Anthropology 4. Viking Fund, New York.

LANNING, EDWARD P.
  1967   *Peru before the Incas.* Prentice-Hall, Englewood Cliffs, N.J.
LATHRAP, DONALD W.
  1970   *The Upper Amazon.* Praeger Publishers, New York.
  1971   "The Tropical Forest and the Cultural Context of Chavin." In *Dumbarton Oaks Conference on Chavin, 1968*, edited by Elizabeth P. Benson, pp. 73–100. Dumbarton Oaks Research Library and Collection, Washington, D.C.
LUMBRERAS, LUIS G.
  1974   *The Peoples and Cultures of Ancient Peru.* Translated by Betty J. Meggers. Smithsonian Institution Press, Washington, D.C.
MACNEISH, RICHARD S., ROBERT K. VIERRA, ANTOINETTE NELKEN-TERNER, AND CARL J. PHAGAN
  1980   *Prehistory of the Ayacucho Basin, Peru, Vol. III: Nonceramic Artifacts.* University of Michigan Press, Ann Arbor.
MALPASS, MICHAEL A.
  1983   "The Preceramic Occupations of the Casma Valley, Peru." In *Investigations of the Andean Past*, edited by Daniel H. Sandweiss, pp. 1–20. Papers from the First Annual Northeast Conference on Andean Archaeology and Ethnohistory, Cornell University, Ithaca.
MASON, J. ALDEN
  1969   *The Ancient Civilizations of Peru.* Penguin Books, Hazell, Watson and Viney Ltd., Aylesbury, Bucks.
MATSUZAWA, TSUGIO
  1978   "The Formative Site of Las Haldas, Peru: Architecture, Chronology, and Economy." Translated by Izumi Shimada. *American Antiquity* 43: 652–673.
MAZESS, RICHARD B., AND D. W. ZIMMERMAN
  1966   "Pottery Dating from Thermoluminescence." *Science* 152: 347–348.
MIDDENDORF, ERNST W.
  1973a   *Perú, Observaciones y Estudios del País y Sus Habitantes durante una Permanencia de 25 Años, La Costa*, vol. 2. Translated by Ernesto More. Universidad Nacional Mayor de San Marcos, Lima.
  1973b   *Perú, Observaciones y Estudios del País y Sus Habitantes durante una Permanencia de 25 Años, La Sierra*, vol. 3. Translated by Ernesto More. Universidad Nacional Mayor de San Marcos, Lima.
MOSELEY, MICHAEL E.
  1975   *The Maritime Foundations of Andean Civilization.* Cummings Publishing Co., Menlo Park.
MOSELEY, MICHAEL E., AND GORDON R. WILLEY
  1973   "Aspero, Peru: A Reexamination of the Site and Its Implications." *American Antiquity* 38: 452–468.
MUJICA, ELÍAS
  1975   "Excavaciones Arqueológicas en Cerro de Arena: Un Sitio Formativo Superior en el Valle de Moche, Perú." Bachelor's thesis, Department of Anthropology, Pontífica Universidad Católica del Perú, Lima.

OLSON, E. A., AND W. S. BROECKER
1959 "Lamont Natural Radiocarbon Dates V." *American Journal of Science* 257: 1–28.
ONERN (OFICINA NACIONAL DE EVALUACIÓN DE RECURSOS NATURALES)
1972 *Inventoria, Evaluación y Uso Racional de los Recursos Naturales de la Costa. Cuencas de los Ríos Casma, Culebras, y Huarmey,* vol. 3. Lima.
OSBORN, ALAN J.
1977 "Strandloopers, Mermaids, and Other Fairy Tales: Ecological Determinants of Marine Resource Utilization—the Peruvian Case." In *For Theory Building in Archaeology,* edited by Lewis R. Binford, pp. 157–206. Academic Press, New York.
PAREDES, VÍCTOR
1975 *Sechín, Posible Centro de Conocimientos Anatómicos y de Disección en el Antiguo Perú.* Gráfica Comercial, Lima.
PARSONS, MARY H.
1970 "Preceramic Subsistence on the Peruvian Coast." *American Antiquity* 35: 292–304.
PATTERSON, THOMAS C.
1971 "Central Peru: Its Economy and Population." *Archaeology* 24: 316–321.
POZORSKI, SHELIA
1976 "Prehistoric Subsistence Patterns and Site Economics in the Moche Valley, Peru." Ph.D. dissertation, University of Texas, Austin. University Microfilms, Ann Arbor.
1979 "Prehistoric Diet and Subsistence of the Moche Valley, Peru." *World Archaeology* 11: 163–184.
1983 "Changing Subsistence Priorities and Early Settlement Patterns on the North Coast of Peru." *Journal of Ethnobiology* 3: 15–38.
POZORSKI, SHELIA, AND THOMAS POZORSKI
1979a "An Early Subsistence Exchange System in the Moche Valley, Peru." *Journal of Field Archaeology* 6: 413–432.
1979b "Alto Salaverry: A Peruvian Coastal Preceramic Site." *Annals of Carnegie Museum of Natural History* 49: 337–375.
1981 "Almejas: Early Exploitation of Warm-Water Shellfish on the North Central Coast of Peru." Ms. in possession of the authors.
POZORSKI, THOMAS
1975 "El Complejo de Caballo Muerto: Los Frisos de Barro de la Huaca de los Reyes." *Revista del Museo Nacional* 41: 211–251.
1976 "Caballo Muerto: A Complex of Early Ceramic Sites in the Moche Valley, Peru." Ph.D. dissertation, University of Texas, Austin. University Microfilms, Ann Arbor.
1980 "The Early Horizon Site of Huaca de los Reyes: Societal Implications." *American Antiquity* 45: 100–110.
1982 "Early Social Stratification and Subsistence Systems: The Caballo Muerto Complex." In *Chan Chan: Andean Desert City,* edited by

        Michael E. Moseley and Kent C. Day, pp. 225–253. University of New
        Mexico Press, Albuquerque.
    1983   "The Caballo Muerto Complex and Its Place in the Andean Chrono-
        logical Sequence." *Annals of Carnegie Museum of Natural History* 52:
        1–40.
POZORSKI, THOMAS, AND SHELIA POZORSKI
    in   "Early Stone Mortars and Bowls from Northern Peru." *Journal of New*
    press a *World Archaeology.*
    in   "Chavin, the Early Horizon, and the Initial Period." In *The Origins*
    press b *and Development of the Andean State*, edited by Jonathan Haas,
        Shelia Pozorski, and Thomas Pozorski. Cambridge University Press,
        Cambridge.
PROULX, DONALD A.
    1968   *An Archaeological Survey of the Nepeña Valley, Peru*. Department of
        Anthropology, Research Report 2. University of Massachusetts,
        Amherst.
    1973   *Archaeological Investigations in the Nepeña Valley, Peru*. Department
        of Anthropology, Research Report 13. University of Massachusetts,
        Amherst.
    1985   *An Analysis of the Early Cultural Sequence in the Nepeña Valley,
        Peru*. Department of Anthropology, Research Report 25. University of
        Massachusetts, Amherst.
QUILTER, JEFFREY
    1985   "Architecture and Chronology at El Paraíso, Peru." *Journal of Field Ar-
        chaeology* 12: 279–297.
RADIOCARBON DATES ASSOCIATION, INC.
    n.d.   Radiocarbon date for Chankillo, sample submitted by H. Reichlen.
RAVINES, ROGGER
    1975   "Garagay, un Viejo Templo en los Andes." *Textual* 10: 6–12.
RAVINES, ROGGER, AND WILLIAM H. ISBELL
    1975   "Garagay: Sitio Ceremonial Temprano en el Valle de Lima." *Revista del
        Museo Nacional* 41: 253–281.
ROE, PETER
    1974   *A Further Exploration of the Rowe Chavin Seriation and Its Implica-
        tions for North Central Coast Chronology*. Dumbarton Oaks Studies in
        Pre-Columbian Art and Archaeology 13. Dumbarton Oaks, Washing-
        ton, D.C.
ROOSEVELT, CORNELIUS VAN S.
    1935   "Ancient Civilizations of the Santa Valley and Chavin." *Geographical
        Review* 25: 21–42.
ROWE, JOHN H.
    1962   "Stages and Periods in Archaeological Interpretation." *Southwestern
        Journal of Anthropology* 18: 40–54.
    1967   "Form and Meaning in Chavin Art." In *Peruvian Archaeology, Se-
        lected Readings*, edited by John H. Rowe and Dorothy Menzel, pp. 72–
        103. Peek Publications, Palo Alto.

SAMANIEGO, LORENZO
1973   *Los Nuevos Trajabos Arqueológicos en Sechín, Casma, Perú.* Larsen Ediciones, Trujillo.
SAMANIEGO, LORENZO, ENRIQUE VERGARRA, AND HENNING BISCHOF
1985   "New Evidence on Cerro Sechin, Casma Valley, Peru." In *Early Ceremonial Architecture in the Andes*, edited by Christopher B. Donnan, pp. 165–190. Dumbarton Oaks Research Library and Collections, Washington, D.C.
SANDERS, WILLIAM T., AND JOSEPH MARINO
1970   *New World Prehistory.* Prentice-Hall, Englewood Cliffs, N.J.
SQUIER, E. GEORGE
1877   *Peru: Incidents of Travel and Exploration in the Land of the Incas.* Harper and Bros., New York.
STRONG, WILLIAM D., AND CLIFFORD EVANS
1952   *Cultural Stratigraphy in the Viru Valley, Northern Peru.* Columbia University Studies in Archaeology and Ethnology 4. Columbia University, New York.
TELLO, JULIO C.
1943   "Discovery of the Chavin Culture in Peru." *American Antiquity* 9: 135–160.
1956   *Arqueología del Valle de Casma, Culturas: Chavín, Santa o Huaylas Yunga y Sub-Chimú*, vol. 1. Universidad Nacional Mayor de San Marcos, Lima.
1960   *Chavín, Cultura Matriz de la Civilización Andina, Primera Parte*, vol. 2. Universidad Nacional Mayor de San Marcos, Lima.
TERADA, KAZUO, AND YOSHIO ONUKI
1982   *Excavations at Huacaloma in the Cajamarca Valley, Peru, 1979.* University of Tokyo Press, Tokyo.
THOMPSON, DONALD E.
1961   "Architecture and Settlement Patterns in the Casma Valley, Peru." Ph.D. dissertation, Department of Anthropology, Harvard University, Cambridge.
1962a "The Problem of Dating Certain Stone-Faced Stepped Pyramids on the North Coast of Peru." *Southwestern Journal of Anthropology* 18: 291–301.
1962b "Additional Stone Carving from the North Highlands of Peru." *American Antiquity* 28: 245–246.
1964a "Formative Period Architecture in the Casma Valley." *Thirty-fifth International Congress of Americanists* 1: 205–212. Mexico City.
1964b "Post-Classic Innovations in Architecture and Settlement Patterns in the Casma Valley, Peru." *Southwestern Journal of Anthropology* 20: 91–105.
1966   "Archaeological Investigations in the Huarmey Valley, Peru." *Thirty-sixth International Congress of Americanists* 1: 541–548.
1974   "Arquitectura y Patrones de Establecimiento en el Valle de Casma." *Revista del Museo Nacional* 40: 9–30.

TOPIC, JOHN, AND THERESA TOPIC
in   "The Archaeological Investigation of Andean Militarism: Some Cau-
press tionary Observations." In *The Origins and Development of the An-
       dean State*, edited by Jonathan Haas, Shelia Pozorski, and Thomas
       Pozorski. Cambridge University Press, Cambridge.

UGENT, DONALD, SHELIA POZORSKI, AND THOMAS POZORSKI
1981   "Prehistoric Remains of the Sweet Potato." *Phytologia* 49 (5): 401–415.
1982   "Archaeological Potato Tuber Remains from the Casma Valley of Peru."
       Economic Botany 36: 182–192.
1983   "Restos Arqueológicos de Tubérculos de Papas y Camotes del Valle de
       Casma en el Perú." *Boletín de Lima* 25: 1–17.
1984   "New Evidence for the Ancient Cultivation of *Canna edulis* in Peru."
       Economic Botany 38: 417–432.
1986   "Archaeological Manioc from Coastal Peru." *Economic Botany* 40:
       78–102.

WICKLER, WOLFGANG, AND UTA SEIBT
1982   "Toad Spawn Symbolism Suggested for Sechin." *American Antiquity*
       47: 441–444.

WILLEY, GORDON R.
1953   *Prehistoric Settlement Patterns in the Viru Valley, Peru*. Bureau of
       American Ethnology, Bulletin 155. Washington, D.C.
1971   *An Introduction to American Archaeology, Volume Two: South Amer-
       ica*. Prentice-Hall, Englewood Cliffs, N.J.

WILLIAMS, CARLOS
1972   "La Difusión de los Pozos Ceremoniales en la Costa Peruana." *Apuntes*
       2: 1–9.
1979–80 "Complejos de Pirámides con Planta en U: Patrón Arquitectónico
       de la Costa Central." *Revista del Museo Nacional* 41: 95–110.
1985   "A Scheme for the Early Monumental Architecture of the Central
       Coast of Peru." In *Early Ceremonial Architecture in the Andes*, edited
       by Christopher B. Donnan, pp. 227–240. Dumbarton Oaks, Washing-
       ton, D.C.

WILSON, DAVID J.
1983   "The Origins and Development of Complex Prehispanic Society in the
       Lower Santa Valley, Peru: Implications for Theories of State Origins."
       Journal of Anthropological Archaeology 2: 209–276.
in   "Reconstructing Patterns of Early Warfare in the Lower Santa Valley:
press New Data on the Role of Conflict in the Origins of Complex North
       Coast Society." In *The Origins and Development of the Andean State*,
       edited by Jonathan Haas, Shelia Pozorski, and Thomas Pozorski. Cam-
       bridge University Press, Cambridge.

Index